3.80

Technology and Survival

Ernest Braun

and

David Collingridge

Technology Policy Unit
University of Aston in Birmingham

Butterworths

LONDON - BOSTON
Sydney - Wellington - Durban - Toronto

B—5

The Butterworth Group

United Kingdom	Butterworth & Co (Publishers) Ltd
London	88 Kingsway, WC2B 6AB
Australia	Butterworths Pty Ltd
Sydney	586 Pacific Highway, Chatswood, NSW 2067
	Also at Melbourne, Brisbane, Adelaide and Perth
South Africa	Butterworth & Co (South Africa) (Pty) Ltd
Durban	152—154 Gale Street
New Zealand	Butterworths of New Zealand Ltd
Wellington	26—28 Waring Taylor Street, 1
Canada	Butterworth & Co (Canada) Ltd
Toronto	2265 Midland Avenue, Scarborough, Ontario, M1P 4S1
USA	Butterworth (Publishers) Inc
Boston	19 Cummings Park, Woburn, Mass. 01801

© SISCON 1977
First published 1977
ISBN 0 408 71301 1

Library of Congress Cataloging in Publication Data

Braun, Ernest, 1925—
    Technology & survival.

    Bibliography: p.
    1. Technology—Social aspects. 2. Human ecology.
I. Collingridge, David, joint author. II. Title.
T14.5.B7   301.24'3   76-56858
ISBN 0-408-71301-1

Typeset by Scribe Design, Chatham, Kent
Printed in England by Chapel River Press Ltd., Andover, Hants.

Preface

In recent years many fears have arisen about the benefits and dangers to society brought about by the increased use of science and technology. It is the purpose of this book to discuss these fears in sufficient detail to obtain an overall view of the field, yet without any pretence at an exhaustive study of the individual causes for concern. The main ingredients of the new fears are all interrelated, but are nevertheless discernible separate strands in a complex pattern.

The first ingredient is the possibility of *exhaustion of natural resources*, including minerals and energy. The consumption of industrial products has seen a meteoric rise over the last three decades and this rise can hardly be sustained without the risk of exhausting finite natural resources. The problem appears to be particularly acute in the demand for energy. While the industrialized world is showing an insatiable appetite for raw materials and energy, the developing world is still suffering from serious shortages of food. The food deficiencies persist despite great science-based improvements in agriculture. Food production can barely keep up with the rate of increase in the world's population.

The *population explosion* is based on great scientific and humanitarian achievements in the control of infectious and insect-borne disease and in the reduction of infant mortality. Science has thus successfully reduced death rates dramatically, but the reduction of birth rates depends much more on social than on scientific factors. Social changes may eventually bring about a reduction in birth rates. For the present, however, the fear of population growth outstripping our ability to supply all the inhabitants of the earth with the bare essentials of existence, is one of the three main causes for doubting the benefits of science.

Population growth is an example of an unintended result of the application of science. Another example which causes much anxiety is *pollution*. This is, in its modern form, an unintended by-product of industrial production, intensive farming and transport. There are many fears about health hazards caused by pollution, about the destruction of wildlife and, finally, about possible damage to the ecosphere. The life-sustaining systems of nature are required to deal with increasing amounts of increasingly complex waste products of civilization. Are our increasing demands for manufactured products causing pollution of the air we breathe and the water we drink beyond recovery? Are our sophisticated technologies destroying the intricate pattern of interdependencies amongst the flora and fauna; are we overheating the earth; are we destroying the natural protection from harmful radiation?

This is the array of fears about the use of science and technology by society: *the exhaustion of natural resources, pollution* and the *growth in population.*

Many solutions to these problems have been proposed and will also be examined, albeit briefly.

The first approach to a solution consists of a critical scrutiny of the criteria used in decisions on technology. The phrase *appropriate technology* has been used to describe this approach. It consists of a wide-ranging assessment of the social, economic and environmental consequences of any proposed technology in order to decide what technology is appropriate for the given situation. In this way harmful consequences should be more readily foreseen and avoided. This approach has led to ideas on intermediate technology, canvassed for use in developing countries.

The second approach consists of an extension of the ideas of intermediate technology to advanced technological societies. This approach calls for a radical re-thinking and re-organization of all our social structures. We would have to move away from the big cities, move away from large-scale industry. Such ideas are discussed in the book *Blueprint for Survival.*

The third solution has been termed the *technological fix.* In a sense it advocates the use of more of the kind of technology we already have, because it believes that problems arising from technology can only be solved by technology. If raw materials are running short, we must improve our methods of extraction. If the population is growing too fast, we must improve methods of contraception. If pollution becomes dangerous, we must improve methods for its control. The hope for the future lies in continuing those improvements that have undoubtedly been made to society by the application of science and technology, while at the same time overcoming difficulties with new and improved technologies.

These are the fears and the proposed solutions which we shall examine. The list is certainly not exhaustive and in particular it omits fears about social instability and about nuclear war. Is the quickening pace of technological change destroying age-old social patterns at a rate to which we cannot adapt? Is the web of society and the psychological make-up of the individual unable to cope with the rapid changes imposed by technology? This kind of question gives rise to the fear that society might become unstable, with social diseases, such as crime, drug addiction and many more, spreading on a large scale. The final fear is that political instability might lead to a major war fought with nuclear weapons, which would virtually wipe out civilized life on earth. These questions are unfortunately beyond the scope of this book.

Note to the teacher

Chapters 1 to 4 should be completed before Chapters 5 and 6 are tackled. Chapters 1 to 3 may be taught in any order, but should all be done before Chapter 4. Chapters 5 and 6 may be done in either order.

Chapter One
The Exhaustion of Natural Resources

World industrial production has been growing at a rate of about 7% per year; a *per capita* rate of increase of about 5% per year (see *Figure 1*). This means of course, a corresponding increase in the consumption of non-renewable natural resources, such as fossil fuels and metal ores, which are used by industry. Some idea of the enormous growth in the consumption of these resources can be obtained from *Figure 2*.

Figure 1   World production of primary commodities and manufactured goods (1948 = 100) (Source: *UN Statistical Yearbooks*)

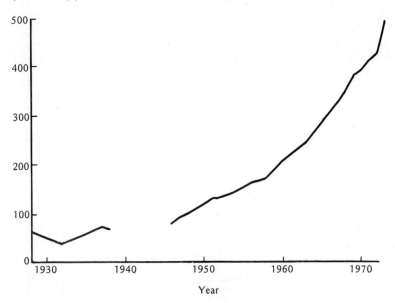

Year

In the first three-quarters of the twentieth century annual consumption of mineral resources, including fuels, has risen by a factor of 14. Consumption of fuels has risen about 15 times, and of petroleum more than 100 times. Steel output has risen 25 times in the same period, and aluminum a startling 1960 times. Consumption of sand, gravel and cement has increased more than 25-fold, whilst even the annual consumption of salt is now more than 12 times what it was at the beginning of the century. Between 1900 and 1950 our consumption of mineral resources greatly exceeded the total consumption of all civilizations before 1900. But such was the growth in

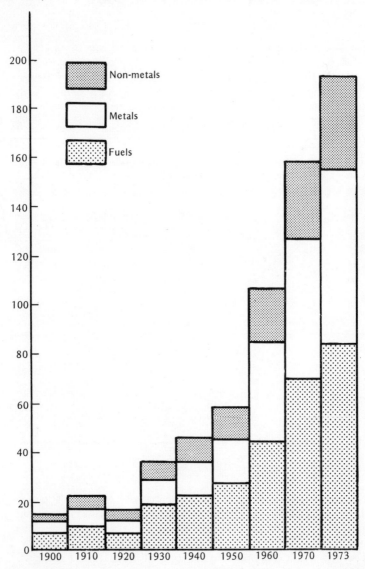

Figure 2 Mineral production in the twentieth century US $ (1972 value) x 10⁹
(Source: A. Sutulov, *Minerals in World Affairs: UN Statistical Yearbooks 1973 and 1974*)

production, that in the next twenty years, even this fabulous consumption was exceeded by some 50%.

The ever-increasing rate of consumption of natural resources has recently given rise to concern about their possible exhaustion. It is very difficult to estimate just how much of a particular resource is available to us, and even more difficult to estimate how long it will take to exhaust whatever quantity exists.

These estimates depend upon a number of factors:

1. *How much of the commodity exists in total throughout the earth's crust, and how it is distributed,* i.e. how much of it exists in a highly concentrated form, and how much in less concentrated forms. Prospecting may always cause these figures to be radically revised. Vast areas of the Soviet Union, for instance, have had no detailed survey for oil.

2. *The economic cost of mining ore and refining it into the final commodity.* An ore is defined as a mineral body from which it is economic to extract a needed material or fuel. At the moment, for example, it is generally economic to extract mercury from rock containing 0.2% mercury, so that any rock with this, or a higher mercury concentration is a mercury ore. A useful way of expressing this is using the 'enrichment factor'. This is the factor by which the metal concentration in the poorest ore exceeds the average concentration of the metal in the earth's crust. The average concentration of mercury in the crust is 8×10^{-6} per cent, which means that a mercury ore must contain at least 25 000 times this concentration. The concentration which can be exploited is, of course, dependent upon the state of technology, as well as a number of other nongeological factors, such as the cost of alternative materials. Enrichment factors for a number of metals with present day technology

Table 1 Enrichment factor for some common metals (from National Research Council, *The Earth and Human Affairs*, p. 80)

Metal	Per cent in crust	Per cent in ore	Enrichment factor
Mercury	0.000008	0.2	25 000
Gold	0.0000002	0.0008	4000
Lead	0.0013	5.0	3840
Silver	0.00007	0.01	1450
Nickel	0.008	1.0	125
Copper	0.006	0.6	100
Iron	5.2	30.0	6
Aluminum	8.2	38.0	4

are given in *Table 1*. Advances in the technology of extraction and in the technology of processing the ore can mean that lower concentrations become usable, i.e. they can lower the enrichment factor. If the enrichment factor for aluminum, at present 4, were reduced to 1, say by developments in the smelting process, then practically any rock could be exploited as aluminum ore.

3

Figure 3 Economics of copper mining in the United States, 1925—1965. (Data from US Bureau of Mines) (from *Resources and Man*, p. 124, National Academy of Sciences, with the permission of W.H. Freeman and Company).

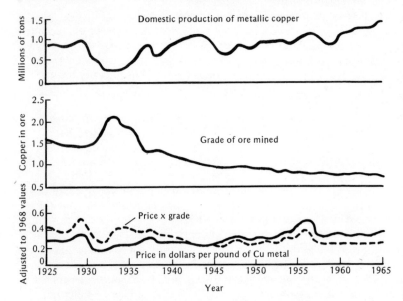

US copper production from 1925—1965 is often used to illustrate this point. *Figure 3* shows that production increased steadily during these years, although the grade of ore exploited decreased sharply. Despite using poorer and poorer ores, technological advances were able to keep the real cost of copper fairly constant.

As lower and lower concentrations of metal ore are exploited, however, the energy consumed in their extraction and processing generally increases. The increase is most marked for the relatively scarce metals, zinc, lead, copper, nickel, tin etc., and less steep for the relatively abundant metals, such as iron and aluminum. Increasing fuel prices are, therefore, likely to have a very marked effect on cost and availability of metals.

3. *The availability and cost of substitutes for scarce materials.* As ever poorer ones need to be exploited, the rich ones having been worked out, the price of the commodity must rise, unless it is offset by technological advance. When the price rises, it becomes worthwhile to search for cheaper substitutes. Substitution of aluminum for copper in electrical products is a good example of this. Although substitution cannot add to the quantity of the original material in the crust, it can greatly extend its life.

4. *The possibility and cost of recycling.* Many metal products can be recycled and the metal they contain recovered and used again.

4

Recycling can be very important. About 40% of US demand for lead, for instance, is met by refining scrap. Figures for iron, copper, mercury and aluminum are 30, 22, 15 and 11 per cent respectively. The amount of material available for recycling depends on a number of factors. For instance, if metal cans were coated with resin which could be burned off, instead of with tin, it would be economic to recycle them. The cost of recycling also depends upon several factors, such as the cost of collecting widely scattered scrap items, and the technology of the recycling process itself. Energy is one commodity that *cannot* be recycled.

5. *The rate of consumption of the resource.* In calculating how long reserves of a particular material are likely to last, we must make assumptions about the rate at which it will be used in the future. This can be extremely difficult, since it depends upon such unknowns as the availability and cost of substitute materials, possible legal restrictions on its use (gold and uranium for instance), and changes in technology, which may eliminate the need for the material.

Great concern about the possible exhaustion of natural resources followed publication of *Limits to Growth* (see Chapter 4). This work showed that known reserves of many important minerals are likely to be exhausted within a very few years. For example, 1970 known reserves of gold, silver, tin and zinc were expected to supply growing world consumption for a further 9, 13, 15 and 18 years respectively (from 1970). This appears to pose a serious problem. Critics of the study have, however, argued that these figures are not as serious as at first they seem, for the following reasons.

1. Known reserves are no indication of how much material will eventually be found to be exploitable, for they refer to deposits which are known and which can be worked with present day technology. The discovery of new deposits can be expected to increase reserves dramatically. Known reserves are necessarily very conservative, for unless there is a shortage, there is no incentive to search for new deposits.

2. As technology enables lower grade ores to be worked, vastly greater quantities of usable material will be open to us. There is obviously more copper in the earth's crust as 0.5% ore than as 1.0% ore. For many important metals an exponential relationship is expected to exist between ore grade and quantity of contained metal.

3. Wealth, or GNP (Gross National Product), can increase without a corresponding increase in the consumption of natural resources. These resources do not, therefore, place a limit on the world's wealth.

Table 2 shows how dependent the rich, industrialized countries are on imports of minerals from poor, underdeveloped countries.

Thus, for example, the poor, third world countries consume only 10% of the copper that they dig from the ground, the rest going to the industrial countries, who manage to produce only about half of their own copper requirements. In recent years the underdeveloped mineral producing countries have shown increasing militancy in demanding more money for their exported minerals. As the lifetime of mineral reserves is reduced, greater exploitation of scarcity by the underdeveloped producers is to be expected.

Optimists see the solution to all these problems as lying in the production of electricity by nuclear power, even though it will be many years before generation by this method could provide a substantial part of the world's electricity (see *Figure 4*). The problems here as we shall see, concern the safety of nuclear reactors, the

Figure 4 World nuclear capacity relative to total electrical capacity (from *Energy in the 1980s*, p. 593 with the permission of the Royal Society)

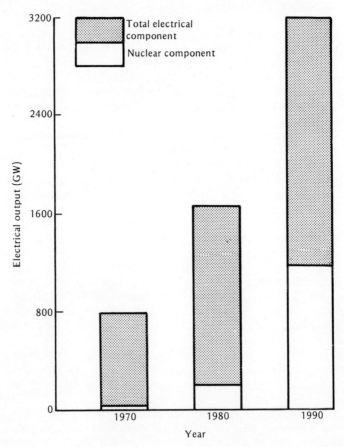

Table 2 Production and consumption of selected mineral commodities: western industrial nations vs the third world (kg *per capita* per year) (from A. Sutulov, *Minerals in World Affairs*, p. 68)

	Third World Countries			Western Industrial Nations		
	Pro-duction	Con-sumption	% use	Pro-duction	Con-sumption	% use
Petroleum	747	184	24.6	897	2039	257
Coal	70	72	103.0	1654	1647	99.5
Iron ore	100	17	17.0	454	669	147.0
Bauxite	18	4.5	25.0	24	55	231
Copper	1.4	0.14	10.0	3.8	7.7	202
Lead	0.4	0.15	37.5	2.5	3.4	136
Zinc	0.6	0.2	36.2	4.5	4.9	108
Nickel	0.1	negligible	4.0	0.5	0.6	120
Tin	0.1	negligible	10.7	negligible	0.2	1150
Steel	13	21	161	560	539	96
Aluminum	0.3	0.27	90	10.6	10.4	98

environmental risks they, and their wastes, represent and the risk of proliferation of nuclear weapons. There are also some doubts about the availability of uranium. If the projection in *Figure 4* is realized, for example, all presently known high grade uranium ores will be exhausted by 1990. Another possible solution to all our energy problems lies in the exploitation of solar energy, which could, theoretically, provide all conceivable energy requirements for as long as the sun lasts. The use of solar energy on a large scale, however, poses some considerable problems. A collector sufficiently large to produce power for a city of one or two million people, about 1000 megawatts, would cover an area of about 15 square miles.

Reading

ESSENTIAL

Bromley, A. and Surrey, A. 'Energy Resources'. In *Thinking about the Future*. Edited by H. Cole *et al.* pp. 90–107
    A good, non-technical, discussion of the problems surrounding estimation of energy reserves, with sections on oil, coal, uranium, and non-conventional hydrocarbons. A guardedly optimistic conclusion is drawn about the future of energy supplies.
Lovering, T. (1969). 'Mineral Resources from the Land'. In *Resources and Man*. (National Academy of Sciences) pp. 109–133. San Francisco, Freeman & Co.
    A discussion of mineral production (excluding energy) covering the problems of estimating reserves, past and future demands, the geography of production and the role of energy in production.

Sutulov, A. (1973). *Minerals in World Affairs.* Chapters 1 and 2, pp. 19–43. Salt Lake City, University of Utah Press
Chapter 1 gives a brief outline of the present state of mineral consumption, putting present consumption into its historical context. Chapter 2 looks at the production of fuels, metals and non-metals and the future of fuel production. The political aspects of trading in minerals and fuels is also touched on.

ADDITIONAL

1. Brooks, D. and Andrews, P. (1974). 'Mineral Resources, Economic Growth and World Population'. *Science,* **185,** 13–19
An optimistic view of the future directed against *Limits to Growth.*
2 Cloud, P. (1969). 'Mineral Resources from the Sea'. In *Resources and Man.* (National Academy of Sciences) pp. 135–155. San Francisco, Freeman & Co.
A look at prospects for extracting minerals (excluding fuels) from sea-water, continental shelves and the deep oceans. The sea will not provide a 'mineral cornucopia', but with skillful invention, it may yield significant quantities of materials.
3. Foley, G. (1975). *The Energy Question.* London, Penguin
An excellent account of energy resources and the problems of finding future sources.
4. Hunt, S. (1974). *Fission, Fusion and the Energy Crisis.* Oxford, Pergamon
A detailed fairly technical account of the physics, economics and safety of nuclear power plants. Chapters 4 and 5 deal with the workings of reactors, Chapter 2 with the physics involved, Chapters 6 and 10 with safety and environmental problems, and Chapters 7 and 8 with the economics of this kind of electricity generation.
5. Maddox, J. (1975). *Beyond the Energy Crisis.* London, Hutchinson
The changes likely to follow the oil crisis will be similar to many other changes which industrial countries have made in the past.
6. National Economic Development Office (1974). *Energy Conservation in the UK.* London, HMSO
A detailed analysis of UK energy consumption, with discussions of how energy may be conserved by each major user. Users considered are domestic, commercial, transport, manufacturing industry, and energy industries. Environmental and social aspects of energy conservation are also considered. The figures it contains may be very useful.
7. Odell, P. (1974). *Oil and World Power.* London, Penguin, 4th edition
The place of energy in world affairs, including an account of the oil crisis of 1974.
8. Patterson, W. (1976). *Nuclear Power.* London, Penguin
A critical history of nuclear power and a very useful statement of the problems which beset it.

9. Steinhart, C. and Steinhart, D. (1974). *Energy, Sources, Use and Role in Human Affairs.* Massachusetts, Duxbury
   A useful history of man's energy use, with an account of energy in natural systems, energy sources and the future of energy supplies.
10. Thring, M. and Crookes, R. (eds) (1974). *Energy and Humanity.* Stevenage, England, Peregrinus
    A very useful collection of articles on future energy needs and supplies.
11. Vernon, R. (ed.) (1976). *The Oil Crisis.* New York, Norton
    Articles on all aspects of the crisis.

Points for discussion or essays

BASED ON ESSENTIAL READING ONLY

(All of these topics can be dealt with using the essential readings only. If, however, it is wished to supplement the essential readings, relevant material from the list of additional reading is given in brackets after each suggestion.)

What is a raw material, and what factors determine whether or not a particular piece of rock is a raw material?

The problems of estimating the reserves of a particular raw material, and the time for its exhaustion.

Likely future developments in the production of minerals and energy. (1, 2, 4, 6, 7, 10, 11)

Why is energy our most important commodity?
Outline its importance in the production process and in the recycling of materials. (9)

It will only be possible to generate large amounts of electricity by nuclear reactors if there is a plentiful supply of uranium, at reasonable prices. What factors determine the availability of uranium and its price? (3, 4, 8)

BASED ON ESSENTIAL AND ADDITIONAL READING

(These topics can only be dealt with using the additional readings as well as the essential ones. The numbers in brackets refer to items on the additional reading list.)

Will it ever be possible to supply most of our energy needs from nuclear reactors? (3, 4, 8)

How much of our energy can we expect to obtain from 'free' sources, such as the sun, the winds and tides, and the earth's heat and running water? (3, 9)

Possible consequences of the dependence of Western countries upon underdeveloped ones for their mineral and energy supplies. (7, 11)

As energy becomes more and more expensive, greater care needs to be used in preventing its waste. What scope is there for energy conservation in the following UK sectors (*to be chosen by the teacher*): domestic, commercial, transport, industry, the energy industries? (6)

What political factors influence world prices for oil? (7, 11)

Chapter Two
Pollution

Introduction

Waste products are the inevitable result of all manufacturing and biological activities. All organisms excrete waste of some kind and in all manufacturing processes waste is produced. It is difficult to define pollution with precision. Taken to an extreme, any impurity in the air we breathe or the water we drink could be called pollution. We shall have to be satisfied with a more operational definition: pollution is the accumulation of waste products or waste energy in the environment to such an extent that damage is done to some human interest. It is obvious that 'damage to an interest' can be open to a wide range of interpretations.

By its very nature, the problem of pollution is as old as mankind. In a low density primitive society, however, the disposal of waste is a simple matter. As the density of population increases, especially in cities, pollution becomes a major problem. Cities have always suffered from it; one only needs to recall accounts of sewage in the streets, infestation by rats, accumulation of horse manure, endemic cholera and air pollution by smoking domestic chimneys.

The reasons for renewed concern about pollution in present day society are threefold:

1. The scale of production, including agricultural production, is such that natural systems, such as rivers, oceans and the air, can no longer cope with the disposal of man-made waste products.
2. The nature of modern wastes is so highly complex that their ill effects cannot be easily predicted, and natural systems cannot cope with the complexity any more than with the total quantity. An enormous range of chemicals, including herbicides and pesticides, as well as radioactive wastes from nuclear plants, fall into this category.
3. The possible result of the combined effects of quantity and complexity of modern wastes could be the destruction of the ecosphere, the web of natural processes which makes life on earth possible. This destruction could consist of long-term changes in the climate or of the entering into food chains of toxic materials. A combination of pollutants may also be the cause of the diseases prevalent in industrial societies.

Classes of pollution

Pollution can be classified according to its origin or type or according

B—5

to the polluted medium. We speak of industrial pollution, automobile pollution, noise pollution etc. It is more common to speak of air pollution, water pollution and land pollution, or to adopt a mixed classification.

AIR POLLUTION

The main components of air pollution are particles of smoke, dust and metals and various gases. Smoke has been eliminated in the UK to a degree by the Clean Air Acts, while dust is an inevitable by-product of tilling the soil. The main components of gas pollution are carbon dioxide, sulfur dioxide and, less concentrated but more toxic, carbon monoxide, and oxides of nitrogen. Air pollution by very fine suspensions of metallic particles, especially lead from car exhausts, is becoming increasingly important. Some attention has recently been focused on pollution of the stratosphere by stable gases, mainly emanating from aerosol cans.

The effects of air pollution on a population can be immediate and drastic. *Table 3*, taken from the fourth report of the *Royal Commission on the Environment,* gives the number of deaths attributed to especially high levels of air pollution during adverse weather conditions on three separate occasions. It is clear that the Clean Air Act has saved lives in Britain.

Table 3 (From 4th Report *Royal Commission on Environmental Pollution,* p. 14 with the permission of HMSO)

Year	Maximum mean daily concentrations in Central London (mg/m^3)		Estimated extra deaths in Greater London
	Smoke	SO_2	
1952	6000	3500	4000
1962	3000	3500	750
1972	200	1200	Nil

It is also generally believed that chronic bronchitis is at least in part associated with air pollution. The death rate from chronic bronchitis in England and Wales in 1963 was 71.3 deaths per 100 000 population; by 1968 the figure had dropped to 57.5. Even this figure compares very unfavorably with the rest of the world (see *The Prevention of Pollution* by R. M. E. Diamant, p. 9).

The emission of lead particles from vehicle exhausts may serve as an illustration of how air pollution is converted into water pollution. The lead particles from exhausts come in varying size — the larger ones settle rapidly on the road surface and are washed away by rain to become water pollutants. The smaller particles become air-borne and are widely dispersed, much like a gas. The extent of harm caused by vehicle exhaust pollution to humans is still controversial, although opinion is beginning to swing towards the view that some harm is done. The possible effects on climate and plants are, of course, well documented in the case of Los Angeles smog (see *The Closing Circle* by B. Commoner, Chapter 3).

LAND POLLUTION

We must make a distinction between unsightly but harmless accumulations of rubbish in the form of tips and litter, and the less apparent but much more dangerous, pollution with waste chemicals. Litter is a social and educational problem, whereas the tipping of municipal waste is growing with the size of cities and the increase in consumption. The average British city dweller now dumps about 1 kg of refuse each day. Much controversy rages about the utilization of this waste. Much of it could be re-cycled if it were properly sorted at source. Much of it could be burnt to provide heating, or thermally decomposed to provide fuel. Very little is used at present. Economic considerations appear to rule against it and it is generally thought that householders could not be asked to sort their waste. Again perhaps a social and educational problem.

The dumping of poisonous wastes has become a matter for concern of late. It is largely carried out on private tips and until recently escaped legislative control in the UK. Recent legislation should improve the situation. The danger of this kind of tipping lies in the exposure of people to the poisonous substances and in their possible seepage into underground water sources.

Perhaps the most difficult problems associated with the disposal of waste on land is associated with radioactive waste from nuclear reactors. All reactors produce large quantities of radioactive waste, consisting in part of very long-lived isotopes. Some of this waste must be kept out of reach of all living creatures for something like a hundred thousand years before it becomes safe to approach. The subject is highly controversial, with opinions ranging over a wide spectrum. At one extreme, experts like Teller assure us that the technology for disposal of this waste is fully developed and perfectly safe. After an initial storage period of perhaps 30 years in cooled stainless steel containers, the radioactive waste can be incorporated into a glassy substance and stored in cooling water for as long as required. Strict security measures must be imposed during this period. At the other extreme, experts like Gofman and Tamplin think that the whole problem of radioactive waste, coupled with the danger of accidents in nuclear plant, is so great that this technology should not be used. Intermediate opinion has it (see Hunt, 1974) that much money and effort needs to be spent on the problem, but that it is basically soluble.

Water pollution, like the pollution of other media, is a complex problem. The sources of fresh water pollution are numerous: industrial effluents discharged either without any treatment or with inadequate treatment; effluent from sewage works; chemicals washed into the waterways by rainfall. There are three main results from all these effluents: lack of dissolved oxygen, the presence of plant nutrients, and the presence of toxic substances.

The lack of oxygen, which is fatal to fish and other aquatic life, is caused, among other things, by raw sewage, wood pulp and excessive growth of algae, produced by phosphates and other plant nutrients in the water. These nutrients are mainly the result of the use of fertilizers, which are eventually washed into the rivers, and the use of detergents with phosphate components.

Nitrates are a common component of effluent from sewage works. The World Health Organization recommends that nitrates in public water supplies should not exceed a concentration of 22.6 ppm of nitrogen. For preference, only half this concentration should be allowed. Excessive nitrate is regarded as a particular danger to bottle-fed infants. Other dangers to health from nitrates are considered

Figure 5   Nitrate concentrations in River Lee and River Thames Quarterly Averages (From 4th Report *Royal Commission on Environmental Pollution*, p. 37 with the permission of HMSO)

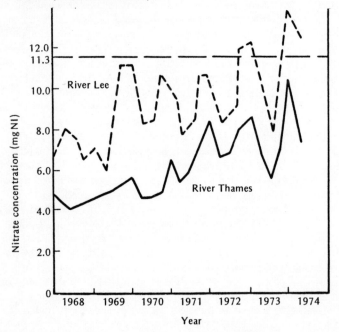

likely. *Figure 5* shows how the nitrate levels in two London rivers behaved over a period of time.

A dramatic case of toxic industrial effluents was reported some years ago when fish in the River Rhine were killed in large numbers. On a smaller scale, these accidents are frequent.

The pollution of estuaries and the sea is of a somewhat different nature. It is known that fish and shellfish can concentrate heavy metals and other pollutants and become a danger to health. A classic case is the poisoning of over a hundred people in Minamata in Japan with mercury, which had become concentrated in fish that they had eaten (see Rothman, 1972 Chapter 9). Sea bathing can become risky in the presence of vast quantities of sewage discharged into the sea. Last, but not least, oil spillages are a major cause of damage to marine life and a major nuisance to those who seek recreation on the beaches.

We shall not attempt to review every kind of pollution in this introductory book. The list of essential reading touches upon most aspects of pollution and the reader is referred to further literature if his interest goes deeper. In the essential reading we have tried to cover the technical aspects of various types of pollution, as well as the great differences in attitude amongst different authors. While the Royal Commission on Environmental Pollution states in para 14 of its fourth report 'We do not accept that pollution will necessarily set a limit to economic growth . . .', authors like Commoner write 'My own judgement, based on the evidence now in hand, is that the present course of environmental degradation, at least in industrialized countries, represents a challenge to essential ecological systems that is so serious that, if continued, it will destroy the capability of the environment to support a reasonably civilized human society . . ..'

The ecosystem

The problem which worries Commoner is the destruction of the ecosystem by pollution. Life can exist only within fairly narrow limits of physical and chemical factors. Organisms cannot exist if the ambient temperature is wrong, if the air is too polluted, if the ozone layer which protects us from ultraviolet radiation from the sun is destroyed, if the soil is too heavily damaged, if pure water is unavailable, etc. In the natural systems which support life and dispose of waste, whether by the action of bacteria or other cyclic processes, there exist many delicate relationships and delicate balances. The life supporting system is called the ecosystem, or ecosphere, and the fear is that pollution may interfere with the delicate web of balances and relationships. For essential details the reader is referred to the book by Commoner, *The Closing Circle.*

As an example of possible damage to the ecosystem we might

discuss the case of carbon dioxide which enters the atmosphere as a result of most combustion processes. The concentration of CO_2 is at present about 320 ppm, and is increasing at a rate of 0.7 ppm per annum. Man-made carbon dioxide now forms an appreciable fraction of the total concentration. It is considered possible that further increases in the concentration of CO_2 could lead to a general warming of the atmosphere, with possibly disastrous consequences. If the average temperature rises sufficiently to cause some melting of the polar ice-caps, large rises in the level of the oceans with consequent flooding would occur. The reason for this fear is that CO_2 absorbs infrared radiation while it passes radiation of shorter wavelengths. This is precisely the property of glass which causes the warming of glasshouses (the so-called glasshouse effect). The argument is largely speculative at the moment. Our knowledge of large scale climatic effects is still quite inadequate to make proper predictions. Nevertheless, this speculation may serve as an indication of the possibly irreversible and catastrophic changes man might cause to the ecosphere if proper care is not taken.

Social and economic aspects of pollution

To explain the peculiar economic nature of the problem of pollution, known as 'externality of costs', we shall quote two paragraphs from the first report of the *Royal Commission on Environmental Pollution:*

> The economic reason why society may not strike the right balance between economic output and the quality of the environment is that the costs of many kinds of pollution are borne not by the polluters, but by somebody else. As a result these 'external' costs will not, in general, be taken fully into account by firms, individuals or other bodies who cause pollution. The other side of the coin is that those who spend money on reducing pollution may not always be the people who gain from the resulting improvement in the environment. This applies both to 'tangible' pollution, such as the poisoning of fish in polluted waters, and to 'intangible' pollution, such as unpleasant smells or ugly landscapes.
>
> Insofar as pollution costs are not borne by those who cause pollution or by the purchasers of their products, but by people who happen to be the victims of the pollution, some of the total welfare resulting from the economic activity of the community is being redistributed away from the victims of pollution in favor of other groups in the community. Manufacturers whose production gives rise to pollution make greater profits

than they would if they were obliged to bear the full social costs of their production, and purchasers of their goods buy them at a lower price than they would if the price had to cover the full social costs involved. Therefore both manufacturers and purchasers gain at the expense of other members of the community who may suffer in one way or another from the pollution.

Clearly, any analysis of the costs and the benefits of reducing pollution must be complex. It is easy enough to say that lethal doses of any toxic substance must never be allowed to accumulate in any place where humans might come into contact with it. But in practice matters are rarely as black and white. Often the real dangers are unknown, often pollution causes a deterioration in the quality of life rather than a hazard to life itself. How much noise are we willing to accept for the sake of cheap mobility on roads and in the air? This is one of many such questions which need much detailed discussion and detailed knowledge.

Barbara Ward and Rene Dubos put it as follows:

> Our understanding of 'external diseconomies' is inherited from an earlier industrial tradition and, today, in virtually all developed economies, whether centrally planned or market economies, it is still the foundation of habitual cost analysis. Modern industrial systems still do not normally include in the cost of what they produce such diseconomies of production and distribution as the spewing off of effluents into the air or the overloading of the land with solid waste or the lack of any charge for eventual disposal of the used-up goods. Thus they pass on a hidden and heavy cost to the community, where it is either met by higher taxation and public spending or by the destruction of amenity.
>
> The costs cannot be avoided. The citizens pay either as consumer or as taxpayer or as victim. The political and economic problems raised by this inexorable and unavoidable price spring from the fact that different citizens are involved in the problem in quite different degrees. The taxpayer may be out of reach of the major pollutions and have no direct incentive to clean them up. Yet poorer citizens can hardly welcome an increase in consumer prices for daily necessities even though they might be glad of cleaner air. The calculus of who shall pay for what improvement is *the* political issue at the core of any policy designed to deal with hidden subsidies and external diseconomies that underlie many of the present methods of satisfying economic needs. (*Only One Earth*, pp. 94–5).

Value judgments are involved at almost all stages of these discussions. What value do we assign to tranquility and what to mobility? In the final analysis these questions become political in the sense that conflicts of interest arise. Different groups within society assign different values, depending on how each of them is affected. The combination of external costs with uncertain values makes for complex political issues. It is for these reasons that many authors regard pollution not so much as a technical problem but mainly a political one. The reader is referred to the book by Rothman for a particular exposition of this view.

Summary

Although pollution is as old as civilization, the intensity and complexity of modern manufacture and agriculture have imposed a new dimension on the problem. For the first time man not only causes localized harm in the form of ugliness, disease and death, but can, by the scale of his activities, upset delicate balances of nature. There is a real possibility of climatic and ecological damage which could conceivably endanger the very existence of civilization.

The solution to the problems of pollution must be in part technical, by finding improved methods of waste disposal and pollution-free production and transportation. In part, however, the solution must come from the political will to face the economic and legal consequences of strict control of pollution.

Reading

ESSENTIAL

Commoner, B. (1972). 'The Environmental Cost of Economic Growth'. In *Energy, Economic Growth and the Environment.* Edited by S. Schurr. pp. 30–65. Baltimore, Johns Hopkins
The author takes a very serious view of pollution, arguing that recent changes in the nature of technology may have already had a dramatic impact on the ecosystem.
Diamant, R. (1974). *The Prevention of Pollution.* Chapter 1. London, Pitman
A statement of the belief that all pollution problems are soluble with sufficient ingenuity.
Rothman, H. (1972). *Murderous Providence.* Chapter 20. London, Rupert Hart Davis
Considers the political and economic aspects of pollution and its control.

1. Abrahamson, D. (1973). 'Ecological Hazards from Nuclear Power Plants'. In *The Careless Technology*. Edited by M. Farrar and J. Millon. Littlehampton, England, Tom Stacey
2. Bain, J. (1973). *Environmental Decay*. Massachusetts, Little, Brown & Co.
   A collection of essays on the economics of environmental control. A useful introduction — the examples are American
3. Commoner, B. (1972). *The Closing Circle*. London, Jonathan Cape
   A very readable book by a leading ecologist. It is really an extended statement of his position in his article quoted above. Most examples are American.
4. Diamant, R. (1974). *The Prevention of Pollution*. London, Pitman
   The emphasis is on the technology of pollution control, with one chapter on legal aspects of pollution in Britain (now a little out of date). A readable, but fairly technical account, of the problems and countermeasures.
5. Hunt, S. (1974). *Fission, Fusion and the Energy Crisis*. Chapter 10. Oxford, Pergamon
   Deals with the environmental problems of nuclear reactors. Takes a middle of the road view.
6. Maddox, J. (1972). *The Doomsday Syndrome*. Chapter 4. London, McGraw-Hill
   The author takes a very optimistic view of pollution and its control. The treatment is at a popular level.
7. Mellanby, K. (1972). *The Biology of Pollution*. London, Edward Arnold
   A short, informative book concentrating on the biological effects of pollution.
8. Mishan, E. (1972). *The Cost of Economic Growth*. London, Pelican
   A readable, non-technical account of the economic problems of pollution, and the inability of traditional economics to deal with them.
9. Rothman, H. (1972). *Murderous Providence*. London, Rupert Hart Davis
   A Marxist view of pollution as an essentially political and economic problem. Contains, nevertheless, much interesting technical detail.
10. *Royal Commission on Environmental Pollution. 1st* and *4th Reports* (1971 and 1974). London, HMSO
    The 1st report is an authoritative review of the pollution problems of the UK, albeit written in official language. The 4th report brings the information in the 1st up to date. On the whole, the Commission is cautiously optimistic.

19

11. *Royal Commission on Environmental Pollution, 6th Report* (1976). London, HMSO
    A thorough study of nuclear power and the environment.
12. Schumacher, E. (1973). *Small is Beautiful.* Part 1, Chapters 3 and 4. London, Blond & Briggs
    A similar position to 8 above. Schumacher argues that traditional economic principles need to be replaced by what he calls 'Buddhist economics'.
13. Southwick, C. (1972). *Ecology and the Quality of our Environment.* London, van Nostrand
    A slightly popular general introduction which considers many social aspects.
14. Tamplin, J. and Gofman, A. (1973). *Poisoned Power.* London, Chatto and Windus
    These authors regard the problems of reactors as virtually insoluble.
15. *The Control of Pollution Act* (1974). London, HMSO
16. *War on Waste* (1974). London, HMSO
    Deals with policies for land reclamation and waste disposal.
17. Ward, B. and Dubos, R. (1972). *Only One Earth.* London, Pelican
    Eminently readable introduction to the whole range of environmental problems. Written for the layman on the occasion of the first UN conference on the environment.
18. Wood *et al.* (1974). *The Geography of Pollution.* Manchester UP
    A detailed and technical discussion of pollution in Greater Manchester. Much useful information on a typical urban environment is given.

Points for discussion or essays

BASED ON ESSENTIAL READING ONLY

(All of these topics can be dealt with using the essential readings only. If, however, it is wished to supplement the essential readings, relevant material from the list of additional reading is given in brackets after each question.)

Is the environmental impact of modern technology qualitatively different from that of earlier technologies? (3)

What role should legislation play in the control of pollution? (4, 9, 10, 15)

Can capitalist societies keep pollution under control? (2, 8, 12, 17)

Discuss *either* pollution by heavy metals *or* pollution from motor vehicles. (4, 7, 10, 17)

(These topics can only be dealt with using the additional readings as well as the essential ones. The numbers in brackets refer to items on the additional reading list.)

Describe the ecosystem, and how man might destroy it. (3, 9)

Discuss the case for and against the use of DDT. (3, 6, 9, 15)

Describe the Los Angeles smog and discuss its effect on US legislation concerning exhaust emissions. (2, 3)

Should we develop nuclear power generation? Discuss the environmental aspects of the problem. (5, 11, 14)

Is pollution likely to set the ultimate limit on economic growth? (6, 8, 9, 15, 16)

Discuss the UK Clean Air Acts, (4, 10) *or* the UK Control of Pollution Act 1974. (15)

Chapter Three
Population

The population explosion

Throughout most of history the human population has been static, or growing very slowly. It has been estimated that until about 1650, population growth averaged only 0.1% per year or less. Sometime after this date, however, the rate of population change began to alter dramatically. By 1750 the rate of increase had perhaps doubled to 0.2% and average growth between 1750 and 1900 was 0.5% per year. From 1900 to 1950 world population growth averaged 1.7% per year, and it is now growing at 2% per year (see *Figure 6*). These figures may seem unspectacular, but a 2% growth rate can have remarkable results over even relatively short times. For instance, if the human race had consisted of only two people at the time of Christ, and had grown steadily at 2% per annum, the world's population would now be 7×10^{16}, with 100 people to each square foot of the earth's surface. In fact, a population growing at 2% per year, doubles in size every 35 years. If the present rate of growth is sustained until the year 2010, the world's population will have doubled, from 3.9 billion (3.9×10^9) to 7.8 billion. If the rate of population growth continues

Figure 6   Population vs Time (from S. Hartley, *Population: Quantity vs Quality*, p. 5)

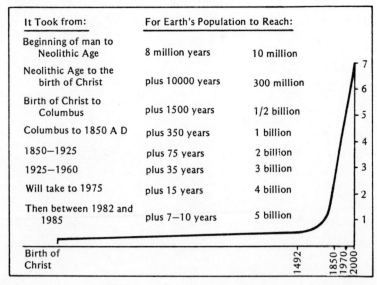

It Took from:		For Earth's Population to Reach:	
Beginning of man to Neolithic Age	8 million years	10 million	
Neolithic Age to the birth of Christ	plus 10000 years	300 million	
Birth of Christ to Columbus	plus 1500 years	1/2 billion	
Columbus to 1850 A D	plus 350 years	1 billion	
1850–1925	plus 75 years	2 billion	
1925–1960	plus 35 years	3 billion	
Will take to 1975	plus 15 years	4 billion	
Then between 1982 and 1985	plus 7–10 years	5 billion	

to increase, as it has done in the past, then this doubling will be achieved in an even shorter period.

So far we have considered only total world population, but the situation begins to look even more serious if we look at population growth on a regional basis. As we shall see later, the early growth in population occurred in Europe, but growth today is concentrated in the poor, so called 'underdeveloped' or 'developing' countries of Africa, Asia and Latin America. In these countries population is growing at between 2.5 and 3.5% per year. As we shall see, these countries are the least well equipped to deal with populations growing at this rate.

To return to world population; if we assume it to be growing at a constant rate, the *absolute* increase in population becomes greater as time goes on. Thus, for example, 1965 saw an extra 65 million people on the planet, whilst 1970 added a total of 72 million. This is equal to the combined population of the UK, Eire, Sweden and Norway. In only 3 years a number equivalent to the present population of the United States will be added to the world's population.

It is, however, difficult to predict future populations. Demographers prefer, therefore, to speak of 'projections' rather than 'predictions'. A projection is a clear-cut calculation of what will happen *if* certain assumptions are satisfied. It is then open to debate whether these assumptions will or will not be satisfied. *Figure 7* gives six recent projections for world population. The UN low, medium and high, all assume some decline in both birth and death rates, although at different speeds, and with the decline beginning at different times. (The birth rate, or fertility of a population is the number of live babies born in one year per 1000 people in the population. The death rate, or mortality, is the number of deaths in one year per 1000 people. Figures for these rates will be found below.) The 2% per year projection, on the other hand, assumes constant birth and death rates. The most extreme projection assumes no decline in birth rate, but a decline in death rate. This produces a population of about 7.5 billion by 2000 AD. The least extreme projection is that of Bogue, who anticipates a strong decline in the birth rate by 1980.

Causes of the explosion

Figure 8 tells us what happened to birth and death rates in European countries after 1800. The horizontal scale is different for different countries, and minor fluctuations have been eliminated. The graph is, therefore, schematic of the changes occurring in Europe after 1800. Until this time both birth and death rates were high, but afterwards the death rate begins to show a steady decline, brought

Figure 7 Six estimates of world population (from *Resources and Man*, p. 55, National Academy of Sciences)

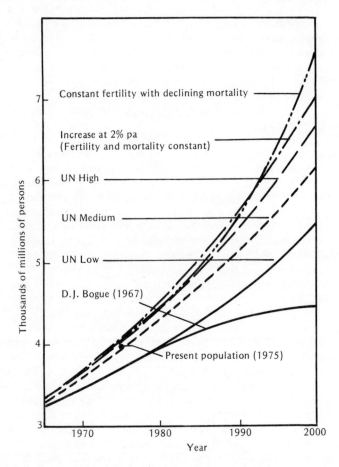

about by increasing agricultural and industrial output, social reforms, improving sanitation and medical care. The birth rate, however, began to fall only some time after the drop in death rate. Thus population grew rapidly for 75–150 years, during which time the population of Europe doubled. This phenomenon is sometimes known as the demographic transition (or, more rarely, the 'demographic revolution'). The transition is from a population with a high death rate and high birth rate, to one where both rates are low.

There is little doubt that the reduction in death rate was the result of better living conditions, although it is difficult to determine the importance of any one factor, such as better hygiene, clean water or increasing food supplies. Why, though, did the fall in birth

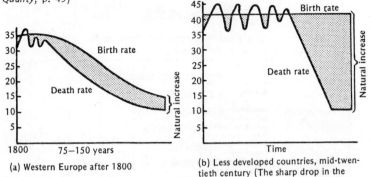

Figure 8 Approximation of the birth and death rates for two different groups of nations over time (from S. Hartley, *Population: Quantity vs Quality*, p. 49)

(a) Western Europe after 1800

(b) Less developed countries, mid-twentieth century (The sharp drop in the death rate began between 1940 and 1960, depending upon the specific country)

rate lag so far behind the decline in the death rate? It is difficult to give a final answer, but one suggestion is as follows. People, before the transition, needed to have many children if they were to leave behind successors, because so many children died in their first few years. As living conditions improved, infant mortality decreased, but people continued to have families as large as in the past, simply out of 'cultural habit'. For this reason the population increased steeply. However, as people became adjusted to the fact that only a few, if any, of their children would die in early life, they came to have smaller families, so that the birth rate fell, eventually coming close to the death rate.

A similar effect is seen in the post-war populations of underdeveloped countries. Here death-rate begins to fall very sharply sometime after 1940, but no corresponding decline in the birth rate is seen (see *Figure 8b*). A huge gap between birth rate and death rate has opened up in these countries with a corresponding enormous increase in population (the shaded area). At present these countries have populations which are increasing at between 2.5 and 3.5% per year. The reduction in death rates in underdeveloped countries, unlike the same reduction in Europe, is *external* to the countries involved, and not related to any significant rise in living standards. The greatest cause has been the introduction of public health measures, such as spraying against insects which carry disease, immunization and treatment with antibiotics. For instance, measures such as the introduction of DDT against malarial mosquitoes reduced the death rate in Ceylon from 22 in 1945, to 10 in 1954. In the decade 1940—50 death rates declined by 46% in Puerto Rico, 43% in Formosa and 23% in Jamaica (see *Figure 9*). Similar improvements in Europe had taken much, much longer — almost 100 years.

25

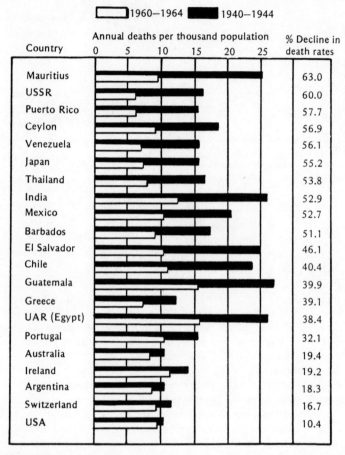

Figure 9 Decline in death rates, 1940–1944 to 1960–1964 (from 'The World Bank Tackles Population', *Population Bulletin*, 34, 3 (November 1968) with the permission of the Population Reference Bureau, Inc, Washington, DC)

The difference between the demographic changes in Europe and those later ones in underdeveloped countries is clearly seen by Jean Bourgeois-Picket, who states:

> The discoveries of sulfa drugs and especially of antibiotics, as well as of insecticides and other means of combating disease-carrying parasites, radically altered the situation. It became possible to lower mortality irrespective of economic development. This was man's first major victory over death. Within a few years, this victory was to be responsible for the rapid population growth that jeopardized the economic growth of the developing areas. The decline in mortality thus became not only

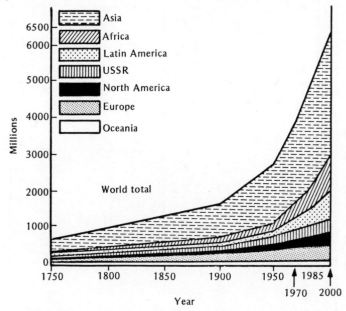

Figure 10   World population, 1750–2000 (from ILO, *Population and Labor*, p. 9)

independent of economic development but a positive obstacle to it. (from *Population Growth and Development*, NY, 1966, p. 61).

Figure 10 shows how the concentration of population growth in the underdeveloped countries is increasing their proportion of the world's population.

Consequences of the population explosion

FOOD

Table 4 shows how world food production has increased in recent years. The production in 1963 is taken as standard, and set at 100. For total production, the change looks very impressive. The table shows, for instance, a 30% increase in food production between 1963 and 1973. This has been achieved at great cost in research and in fertilizer and pesticide applications. If we look at the *per capita* figures, however, things are quite different. In the period covered by the table, world population has risen by 20%. When the food production of 1973 is distributed over the world's population, the *per capita* food production has increased by only 9%. In other words, the

27

Table 4 Total and *per capita* food production 1961–1973, by regions, 1963 = 100 (Source: *UN Statistical Yearbooks, 1973 and 1974*)

Regions	1961	1962	1964	1965	1966	1967	1968	1969	1970	1971	1972	1973
A. total food production												
World	95	93	104	105	110	114	118	119	122	126	126	130
Africa	91	96	100	102	102	109	111	116	119	125	126	121
America, North	92	95	100	103	107	112	113	113	111	121	120	123
America, Latin	95	96	103	108	109	115	116	121	126	128	129	132
Asia												
Near East	92	99	104	105	110	115	120	122	125	130	139	134
Far East	96	97	103	101	101	107	114	118	123	123	120	130
Europe												
Eastern and USSR	101	104	110	110	125	126	132	129	136	139	140	153
Western	93	99	102	102	105	112	114	114	116	121	120	123
Oceania	89	98	105	99	114	104	126	120	119	126	124	126
B. *per capita* food production												
World	99	100	102	101	103	105	107	106	106	108	106	109
Africa	95	98	98	97	95	99	99	100	100	102	101	95
America, North	95	96	99	101	103	107	106	105	102	111	108	109
America, Latin	101	99	100	102	100	103	101	102	103	102	100	100
Asia												
Near East	97	102	101	100	102	104	105	104	103	104	108	101
Far East	100	100	101	96	95	98	101	102	104	102	97	101
Europe												
Eastern and USSR	104	105	109	108	121	121	125	122	127	129	129	140
Western	95	100	101	100	102	108	110	108	110	114	112	114
Oceania	92	100	103	95	108	97	115	103	104	109	105	113

enormous effort of increasing the total amount of food in the world is almost nullified by the increase in population. However, the figures become even worse when examined on a regional basis, for it is then seen that most of the increase in production has occurred in the rich, developed countries, and not in the underdeveloped ones. In the Far East, for example, food production has shown a 30% increase between 1963–1973, but population has grown so rapidly that the food *per capita* has remained roughly constant. As Kenneth Boulding has remarked:

> . . . . any technological improvements will have the ultimate effect of increasing the sum of human misery, as it permits a larger population to live in precisely the same state of misery and starvation as before the change. ('The Utterly Dismal Theorem' in *Population, Evolution and Birth Control*, ed. G. Hardin, p. 81).

To obtain some idea of the disparity between diets in the rich and poor countries, consider that if the world's food were parcelled out at the average dietary level of the USA, only one third of the human race could be fed. Something like half of the world's population are either hungry as a matter of normal existence (undernourished), or exist on a seriously unbalanced diet (malnourished). Some 20% of people in underdeveloped countries are undernourished, and 60% are malnourished. The most unfortunate are those who are both under-nourished and malnourished, i.e. those who receive an inadequate quantity of unbalanced food. The commonest form of malnutrition is a general deficiency of protein and/or calories (protein-calorie malnutrition, or PEM, or PCM). There are two principal manifesta-tions of the disease, both commonest in young children; marasmus, characterized by emaciation, and kwashiorkor, in which fluid accumulates in the tissues, giving the sufferer a characteristically swollen appearance. But perhaps the gravest result of a deficient diet in children is an irreversible reduction in mental ability.

DISTORTION OF POPULATION STRUCTURE

In a rapidly growing population the proportion of young people in the population increases. Thus, in Cost Rica, a country which shows one of the greatest increases in population, one-half of the population is under 15. *Figure 11* shows typical population structures for developed (low fertility) countries and underdeveloped (high fertility) countries.

There are two serious consequences of this distortion in popula-tion structure. Young people contribute little to the wealth of their community. Instead they are net consumers of wealth because they have to be fed, clothed and sustained by the work of others. Rapid

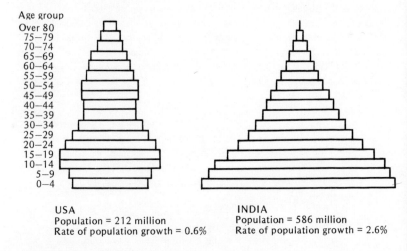

Figure 11 Population structure: high and low fertility countries (Source: *UN Demographic Yearbook 1974*)

Age group
Over 80
75–79
70–74
65–69
60–64
55–59
50–54
45–49
40–44
35–39
30–34
25–29
20–24
15–19
10–14
5–9
0–4

USA
Population = 212 million
Rate of population growth = 0.6%

INDIA
Population = 586 million
Rate of population growth = 2.6%

population growth, therefore, places a great burden on those of working age. There is the need to educate the growing numbers of young people. So far underdeveloped countries have made great efforts in education. For instance, the number of primary school pupils in these countries increased by 150% from 1950 to 1965, and the percentage of all children between 6 and 12 who were in schools rose from less than 40% to more than 60%. Yet the strains produced by a growing population threaten to overwhelm these efforts. Between 1960 and 1970 the *absolute* number of illiterate people in underdeveloped countries *rose* by some 70 million.

Figure 12 gives a measure of the problem in terms of 'dependency ratio'. It is assumed that the productive life of a person is from 15 to 64. The 'youth dependency' is then defined as the ratio between the number of people under 15 to each 100 people between 15 and 64. 'Age dependency' is similarly defined as the number of people over 64 for every 100 people between 15 and 64. Total dependency is the sum of these two figures.

UNEMPLOYMENT AND UNDEREMPLOYMENT

A man or woman is unemployed if he or she is able to work, but is not doing so. Underemployment occurs when too many people are employed on a task, so that the removal of one person from the work force has no real effect on the amount of work done. Unemployment in underdeveloped countries is a very serious problem. Because of their high rate of population growth, not enough non-agricultural jobs are available to the growing labor force, and because of small

Figure 12 The dependency load for various countries (Source: *UN Demographic Yearbook 1974*)

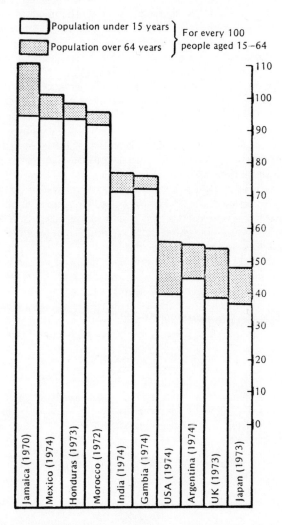

landholdings, adding to the agricultural labor force generally creates underemployment.

THE GROWING CITIES

Mostly as a result of rural unemployment, the cities in underdeveloped regions of the world have been growing at an alarming rate. Various projections put the population of Calcutta in 2000 as between 36 and 66 million! Its present population is around 7 million, crowded into an area of 490 square miles. Three-quarters of the present population live in tenements, slums and shanty towns, and half have 30 square feet of living space or less per person. The migration which has created these problems has also produced a great imbalance between the sexes; there are nearly twice as many men as women in Calcutta. According to the Calcutta Metropolitan Planning Organization (1966):

> Calcutta is a city in crisis. All who live in this huge metropolitan complex have daily experience of its characteristic problems; chronic deficits in basic utilities such as water supply, sewerage and drainage; and in community facilities such as schools, hospitals, parks and recreation spaces; severe unemployment and underemployment, congested and inadequate transportation; vast housing shortages and proliferating slum areas; soaring land prices and rents; administrative delays and confusion of responsibility for corrective action; absence of clear development objectives over a longer perspective than the next 5 year plan; limited state and municipal financial resources to cope with the situation.
>
> Over the past two hundred years many boards and committees and commissions have met and deliberated on the problems of the city and issued reports calling for remedial action. The improvements that were made, if indeed any action was taken, were invariably piecemeal, sporadic, and inadequate to meet the needs of the rapidly increasing population of Calcutta.

THE GROWING GAP BETWEEN RICH AND POOR

It is difficult for poor, underdeveloped countries to find the money needed for investment to raise the *per capita* wealth of their populations. The difficulty is compounded by the growing population, since the new wealth created by investment must be shared out amongst ever greater numbers. Thus, for example, the countries of Latin America achieved an increase in gross domestic product (GDP)

Table 5   Gross domestic product *per capita* (US $ 1974 value) (Source: *UN Statistical Yearbook 1974*)

Sweden (1974)	6185	Turkey (1974)	546
USA (1974)	6167	Brazil (1972)	513
Denmark (1974)	5481	Zambia (1972)	386
Japan (1974)	3782	Paraguay (1974)	373
Australia (1972)	3730	Peru (1972)	372
Israel (1974)	2883	Ghana (1972)	233
UK (1972)	2471	Bolivia (1972)	221
Venezuela (1974)	1580	Ceylon (1972)	174
Argentina (1971)	1260	Pakistan (1972)	116
Chile (1972)	649	India (1970)	99
Iran (1972)	571	Ethiopia (1972)	80

of 6.2% per annum, between 1960 and 1968, but because of the region's increasing population this amounted to an increase of *per capita* GDP of only 3.2% per annum.

Since the increase in GDP *per capita* in underdeveloped countries was less than the increase in *per capita* GDP in the developed countries, the gap between the standard of living in the developing and in the developed world increased. *Table 5* gives the GDP *per capita* for various countries. The richest, Sweden, is, by this measure, nearly 77 times wealthier than the poorest, Ethiopia.

Reading

ESSENTIAL

Ehrlich, P. and Ehrlich, A. (1970). *Population, Resources, Environment.* San Francisco, Freeman & Co.
Chapter 2 (pp. 5–24) gives a history of population growth and the factors affecting it. Chapter 3 (pp. 25–49), the age structure of populations and the factors determining it, distribution of earth's population, urbanization and the problems of projecting future populations. Chapter 4 (pp. 65–77 only), malnutrition and undernutrition in underdeveloped countries.

ADDITIONAL

1. Allaby, M. (1972). *Who Will Eat?* Prospect for Man Series
   This is an important book on the world food problem. The author is a soil scientist and is therefore concerned mainly with the agricultural and economic aspects of the problem.

   He documents many of the ecological side effects of the 'Green Revolution' and criticizes the approach of the 'technophiles' who believe that the application of ultramodern technology can solve anything. He discusses and dismisses many of the technological solutions which have been put forward for dealing with our expanding population (like the suggestion that other planets should be colonized) and puts forward a compelling case for world cooperation in immediate stabilization and, in some areas, reduction of population and the development of technologies and a way of life which minimally disturbs the ecosystem.
2. Bairoch, P. (1973). *Urban Unemployment in Developing Countries.* Geneva, International Labor Office
   A report resulting from the ILO's World Employment Program. A thorough study of the size of the problem, its causes and remedies, with useful references.

3. Bardhan, K. and Bardhan, P. (1973). 'The Green Revolution and Socio-Economic Tensions: the case of India'. *International Social Science Journal*, **25**, 3, pp. 285–292
   Argues that the Green Revolution has accentuated the gap between the rich and poor in underdeveloped countries — a gap which was already enormously wide. The Green Revolution may change its color to red.
4. Borlaug, N. (1971). 'The Green Revolution: For Bread and Peace'. *Bulletin of the Atomic Scientists*, June, pp. 6–9 and 42–48.
   A brief account of the Green Revolution by one of its principals.
5. Cassen, R. (1974). 'Economic–Demographic Interrelationships in Developing Countries'. In *Population and its Problems*. Edited by H. Parry. Oxford, Clarendon Press, pp. 216–243
   A thorough discussion of the economic factors determining population size and growth, using India as a case-study. Family planning programs can succeed only when accompanied by reducing infant and child mortality, improved education and living conditions, and higher employment rates. Economic planning in underdeveloped countries should aim to provide the socio-economic conditions which encourage the demographic tradition. A useful reference source.
6. Donaldson, P. (1973). *Worlds Apart*. London, Penguin
   A layman's guide to the economic and social needs of developing countries, and the growing gulf between the rich and the poor countries of the world.
7. Ehrlich, P. and Ehrlich, A. (1970). *Population, Resources, Environment*. San Francisco, Freeman & Co.
   Chapter 5 (pp. 81–116) a discussion of ways in which food production might be increased. Chapter 9 (pp. 211–232) techniques of birth control, their advantages and disadvantages, failure rates, etc. Chapter 10 (pp. 233–258) family planning in the developed and in the underdeveloped countries. Factors determining family size in both are discussed. Appendix 2 gives population estimates for regions of the world 1960–2000 on UN high, low, medium and constant-fertility–no-migration variants.
8. Hartley, S. (1972). *Population: Quantity or Quality*. New Jersey, Prentice-Hall
   An excellent book on all aspects of the population problem. The problem is treated in some depth, but in non-technical language. Strongly recommended. It also contains a very good bibliography.
9. Hendricks, S. (1969). 'Food from the Land'. In *Resources and Man*. (National Academy of Sciences) pp. 65–85. San Francisco, Freeman & Co.
   A detailed account of the prospects for producing more food by traditional agriculture. A 'rule of two' is concluded, allowing food

production to double by the introduction of new lands, by
increased productivity, and by innovation, giving a possible eight-
fold increase altogether.

10. International Labor Office (1973). *Population and Labor.* Geneva
    A good, non-technical account of the employment problems
    generated by the population explosion. The book contains a
    useful guide to further reading.
11. Meadows, D. *et al.* (1972). *The Limits to Growth.* London, Earth
    Island Ltd, pp. 45—54
    A brief discussion on the amount of land that might be brought
    into agricultural production, and the costs involved.
12. Mesarovic, M. and Pestel, E. (1975). *Mankind at the Turning Point.*
    London, Hutchinson, Chapters 5 and 9.
    Using a model of the world the authors make projections about
    food production, population and development aid policies.
13. *New Scientist* (1974). **64**, 922, 7th November, pp. 388—411,
    special issue on 'The Hungry Planet'.
    An issue coinciding with the UN World Food Conference in Rome.
    A generally pessimistic view is taken. Titles are: M. Allaby,
    Fertilizers - The Holes in the Bag; R. Allen, Turning Platitudes
    into Policy; M. Muller, Aid, Corruption and Waste; P. Payne,
    Protein, Deficiency or Starvation?; J. Tinker, The Green Revo-
    lution is Over.
14. Pimentel, D. (1973). 'Food Production and the Energy Crisis'.
    Science, **182**, pp. 443—449
    Agriculture is only managing to achieve greater yields at the cost
    of consuming more and more energy — there are some startling
    figures on this point. Energy costs will have an even greater effect
    on food production in the future as oil becomes scarcer. 'We
    wonder if many developing countries will be able to afford the
    technology of US agriculture.'
15. Ricker, W. (1969). 'Food from the Sea'. In *Resources and Man*
    (National Academy of Sciences) pp. 87—108. San Francisco,
    Freeman & Co.
    A detailed discussion of how the oceans and inland waters might
    yield more food. His conclusion is that they can provide only a
    limited quantity of food for the earth's population.
16. Wade, N. (1974). 'Green Revolution I and II'. *Science*, 20th Dec.
    and 27th Dec., pp. 1093—1096 and 1186—1192
    A general, and balanced survey of the Green Revolution — its
    successes and its failures.
17. Young, L. (ed.) (1968). *Population in Perspective*, Part III. London,
    Oxford University Press
    Contains statements of the various religious views on birth control,
    sex and family life.

Points for discussion or essays

BASED ON ESSENTIAL READING ONLY

(All of these topics can be dealt with using the essential reading only. If, however, it is wished to supplement the essential reading, relevant material from the list of additional reading is given in brackets after each question.)

Discuss the relationships between fertility, mortality and the age distribution of population. What problems are created by different age distributions? (2, 5, 8, 10)

Discuss the causes of worldwide population increase from about 1800 to the present. (5, 7, 8)

Compare the growth in overall population, and in urban population, in Europe and in underdeveloped countries from 1800 to the present. (2, 5, 7, 8, 10)

Why has the demographic transition not yet occurred in most underdeveloped countries? Is it likely to occur in the near future? (5, 7, 8)

Gunnar Myrdal urges that all development studies must be based upon the moral imperative that:

> any attempt to depress population growth is restricted to work on the fertility factor. Complacency about or even tolerance of a high level of mortality because it slows down population growth is simply not permissible. (*The Challenge of World Poverty*, p. 152)

The opposite view is expressed by John D. Black

> Another point of view is that of the pure unthinking sentimentalist who says that relieving hunger and disease is always good and that it is the moral obligation of other nations to do this . . . . The answer is that, when whole populations are considered, prolonging a few lives this year is of no avail if this causes more misery and suffering in the years following . . . . Those who speak in this way are charged with being 'hard boiled' and non-humanitarian, but they are the true humanitarians. ('The Economics of Freedom from Want' *Chronica Botanica*, 1948).

Consider these two opposed views.

BASED ON ESSENTIAL AND ADDITIONAL READING

(These topics can only be dealt with using the additional readings as well as the essential one. The numbers in brackets refer to items on the additional reading list.)

Why has the food *per capita* produced by the underdeveloped countries not increased significantly over the past decade? (4, 6, 7, 8, 9, 13, 16)

Will the shortage of cheap energy place a limit on the quantity of food which the world can produce? (4, 13, 14, 16)

Why has the economic gap between the wealthy, developed countries and the poor, underdeveloped countries increased? Will it continue to increase, and should this be a cause of concern to us who live in the developed world? (6, 8, 12)

What are the Roman Catholic Church's arguments against birth control, and what do you think of them? (17)

Why is the provision of cheap, effective and socially acceptable contraceptives not the solution to the population problem in underdeveloped countries? (5, 6, 7, 17)

Chapter Four
Limits to Growth?

Introduction

So far we have discussed three problems related to the use of science; the exhaustion of natural resources, pollution of the environment, and population growth. Although we have treated these problems in separate chapters and have given little attention to the relations between them, it is obvious that they are not independent of each other.

The best known attempt to link together the three problems we have discussed is due to Meadows and his colleagues (*Limits to Growth*). Meadow's team studied the interactions between the three problems by means of a highly complex mathematical model which they used to forecast future trends. Although their results, and even their methodology, have by now been seriously questioned, it is worth studying their work, for it shows how complicated the real relationships between our three problems must be. In fact, the relationships are so complex, and the uncertainties so large that it is probably impossible to make accurate forecasts of future levels of pollution, population or the availability of natural resources. (For discussion of the difficulties, see the Sussex University study, *The Art of Anticipation*, and also *Thinking about the Future*, their critique of Meadows' work.)

The most important concept in any model linking various factors is a feedback loop. The feedback loop in *Figure 13* describes the relationship between industrial capital in use, and so industrial output, and investment and depreciation. The capital invested depends upon industrial output, which generates all capital, and the fraction of this capital which is ploughed back into industry (the investment rate). With a fixed rate of investment, the greater industrial output, the greater the amount invested, and the more that is invested, the greater the industrial output. This is known as a positive feedback loop. Left unchecked, it leads to exponential growth, more output producing more investment, and more investment producing more output. The only check on this growth is the obsolescence of capital goods such as machinery, factories, roads and so on. The faster this depreciation of capital, the less capital there is for generating industrial output. The less capital output, the less industrial capital and so the less depreciation of capital. There is, therefore, a negative feedback loop between capital and depreciation. The strength of this loop depends upon the rate of depreciation.

Such positive and negative feedback loops can be seen behind many quantities. The size of a population, for example, depends upon the positive feedback loop of births and the negative feedback loop of deaths as shown in *Figure 14*. Feedback loops can be much more complex and roundabout than the simple ones described so far. *Figure 15* shows how industrial capital might be related to population.

Figure 13   **Feedback loops for industrial capital** (from *Limits to Growth*, p. 39)

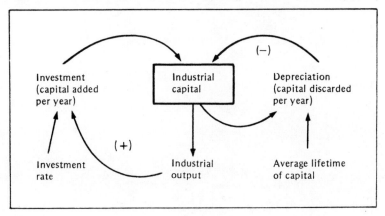

Figure 14   Feedback loops determining population

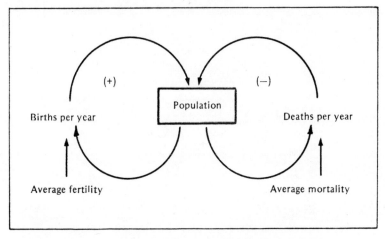

Figure 15 consists of a whole series of feedback loops, linked together in a complicated way. Those loops which are always positive or always negative are marked (+) and (−). Unmarked loops may be either positive or negative, depending on what assumptions are made. Let us consider some of the paths connecting industrial capital with population.

39

Figure 15 Feedback loops of population, capital, agriculture and pollution (from *Limits to Growth*, p. 97)

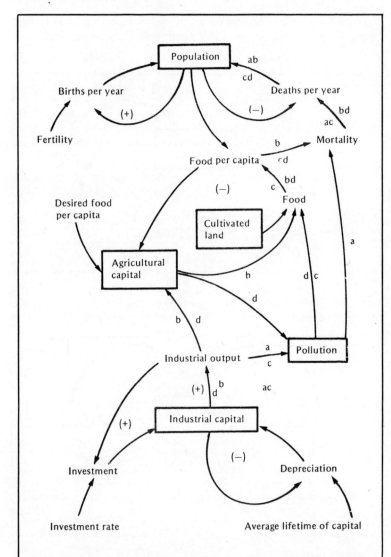

Some of the interconnections between population and industrial capital operate through agricultural capital, cultivated land, and pollution. Each arrow indicates a causal relationship, which may be immediate or delayed, large or small, positive or negative, depending on the assumptions included in each model run.

(a) An increase in industrial capital produces an increase in industrial output, which produces more pollution. This produces a rise in mortality, which tends to reduce the population.

(b) An increase in industrial output may also lead to an increase in agricultural capital, the wealth tied up in producing food, (farmland, tractors, fertilizers etc.), which will increase the amount of food produced. This increases food *per capita*, which reduces mortality, thus increasing the population.

(c) In (a), an increase in industrial capital leads to an increase in pollution which reduces population by increasing mortality. Pollution can, however, affect population in another way — by causing a direct decrease in the amount of food grown. Whether or not the increased pollution produces an increase or a decrease in food *per capita* depends upon which of these loops is strongest.

(d) Industrial output, when increased, leads to a growth in agricultural capital, which can cause an increase in pollution (through pesticide misuse and fertilizer run-off for example), with a corresponding decrease in the quantity of food produced, and a consequent decline in population. This loss in production may or may not exceed the increase in agricultural production brought about by growth in agricultural capital.

We can see, then, that the relationship between industrial capital and population is extremely complex. It is best to think of it, not as one relationship, but as a whole network of relationships. *Figure 15* represents a *model*, or mathematical description, of these relationships between population, industrial and agricultural capital and pollution. It is obviously very difficult to predict what will happen to any particular quantity in the model, say, population, when another quantity, say agricultural capital, is altered. To begin with, all the relationships in the model must be quantified and when this is done, the calculations involved are enormously complex. In fact, they can only be performed by a computer.

The principal quantities (or levels) which figure in the Meadows model are industrial capital, population, food production, pollution and the consumption of non-renewable resources. The model

> . . . is simply an attempt to bring together the large body of knowledge that already exists about cause-and-effect relationships between the five levels . . . and to express that knowledge in terms of interlocking feedback loops. (*Limits to Growth*, p. 90)

Having constructed the model Meadows' team could use it to make various projections about the future. In other words, certain assumptions were fed into the model and their consequences for the future calculated. It was not the team's job to *predict* the future, but merely to say what *would* happen in the future *if* a particular set of assumptions are satisfied. Some of the more important results obtained from the model are discussed below.

Results from the model

STANDARD RUN

Here it is assumed that no major changes occur in the relationships which have historically governed the development of the world system, and results for future levels for the five principal quantities are predicted. (In all diagrams vertical scales are omitted in order to emphasize the general behavior of the model, and because quantitative data is often missing. Scales are identical, however, on all diagrams).

Results of the standard run are shown in *Figure 16*. As industrial output increases, resources are consumed at an ever increasing rate, leading to increased costs for materials, as poorer and poorer ores are used. As resource prices rise, more and more capital must be spent on acquiring raw materials, and less is left for investment for future growth. Eventually investment cannot keep up with depreciation and

Figure 16 World model standard run. All variables follow historical values from 1900 to 1970 (from *Limits to Growth*, p. 124)

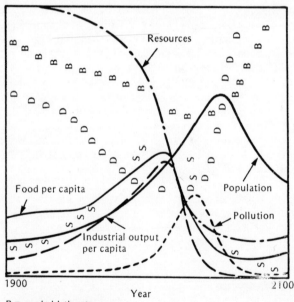

B = crude birth rate
D = crude death rate
S = services *per capita*

the industrial base collapses, leading to a final decrease in population, when the death rate is increased by lack of food, due to lack of investment in agriculture, and decline in health services.

'UNLIMITED' RESOURCES

Since the problem with the standard run was depletion of resources, the team used the same assumptions as before, except that they now assumed that cheap nuclear power is available, which would double the reserves of all resources (by making it economically possible to exploit very low grade ores), and which would allow extensive recycling of materials. The result of these assumptions is shown in *Figure 17*. Here growth is eventually halted by increased pollution from the growing industry, which causes an increase in mortality and a decrease in food production.

Figure 17   World model with 'unlimited' resources (from *Limits to Growth*, p. 132)

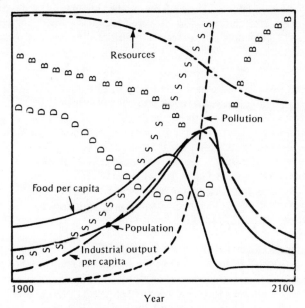

'UNLIMITED' RESOURCES AND POLLUTION CONTROLS

The next step is obviously to see if introducing pollution controls into the world model will prevent its collapse. What now happens is that population and industry grow until the limit of arable land is reached, leading to a decline in food *per capita*, and a decline in industrial growth as more and more capital has to be invested in agriculture.

43

'UNLIMITED' RESOURCES, POLLUTION CONTROLS, AND INCREASED AGRICULTURE

The question now is whether the collapse of the model can be avoided by increasing food production. It is therefore assumed that average land yield is doubled in 1975. This removes so many constraints on growth that population and industrial output reach very high levels, so much so that pollution eventually brings about collapse of the model. The model incorporates strict pollution controls, so that pollution per unit of production is low, but production rises to such high levels that the total quantity of pollution is large enough to seriously increase mortality and decrease food production.

'UNLIMITED' RESOURCES, POLLUTION CONTROLS, INCREASED AGRICULTURE AND PERFECT BIRTH CONTROLS

Adding controls on population, in the form of 'perfect' birth control, does not prevent the collapse of the model. Population is stabilized, and average income *per capita* rises to a high level, but a combination of resource depletion and increasing pollution finally leads to collapse.

A STABLE MODEL

Meadows' team found that the only way to construct a stable model which avoided collapse was to add to the assumptions above a limit on industrial production, thus reducing resource consumption and pollution levels. The stable model contains the above assumptions plus others, amongst which are the following:
1. The population has access to 100% effective birth control.
2. The average desired family size is two children.
3. Industrial output *per capita* is restricted to its 1975 value.

Natural delays in the model then allow population and industrial output *per capita* to gradually approach stable, constant levels (*Figure 18*).

It was found that if the policies needed for the stable model were delayed from 1975 to 2000, then the model became unstable once more. Population and industrial output rise to levels too high to be sustained, leading to food and resource shortages before 2100.

According to *Limits to Growth* (pp. 173–174), the minimum set of requirements for the state of global equilibrium are:
1. The capital plant and the population are constant in size. The birth rate equals the death rate and the capital investment rate equals the depreciation rate.
2. All input and output rates — birth, deaths, investment, and depreciation — are kept to a minimum.
3. The levels of capital and population and the ratio of the two are set in accordance with the values of the society. They may be

Figure 18   Stabilized world model I (from *Limits to Growth,* p. 165)

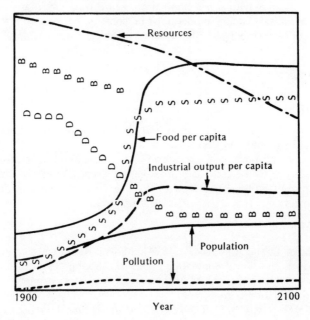

deliberately revised and slowly adjusted as the advance of technology creates new options.

Criticisms of *Limits to Growth*

The construction of a world model such as that used by Meadows obviously involves a great many assumptions, about what relationships exist, and about what values should be attached to these relationships. Meadows' model has been criticized for the assumptions it makes, the most detailed criticism to date being that of the Science Policy Research Unit at Sussex University, published in *Thinking About the Future.* There seem to be six major criticisms of the model.
1. It lacks economic feedback loops working through market forces.
2. The quantitative assumptions about the relationships between pollution and mortality, and pollution and food production are far too pessimistic.
3. Available mineral resources have been seriously underestimated, by considering only reserves that are presently workable. As technology advances, poorer grades of ore will be usable.
4. The model fails to allow for technological improvements.
5. The fertility model is poor, and based upon inadequate data.

45

6. It is misleading to lump the entire world together, as the model does, dealing with *world* population, *world* food production and so on. A satisfactory model must be constructed so as to reflect the difference between the different regions of the world.

Reading

ESSENTIAL

Meadows, D. *et al.* (1972). *The Limits to Growth.* London, Earth Island Ltd and Pan Books (1974).
This is a non-technical exposition of the Meadows' model. Full references to the technical literature are given. Chapter I - The Nature of Exponential Growth. II - The Limits to Exponential Growth. V - The State of Global Equilibrium.

ADDITIONAL

1. Brooks, D. and Andrews, P. (1974). 'Mineral Resources, Economic Growth and World Population'. *Science*, **185**, pp. 13–19
An optimistic account of future natural resources, strongly critical of *Limits to Growth.*
2. Cole, H. *et al.* (1973). *Thinking About the Future.* London, Chatto & Windus
An extended critique of *Limits to Growth.* Some of the chapters are too technical to be of much use to students, unless they have a special interest in modelling. The following are, however, useful: Chapter 3 - The Non-Renewable Resources Sub-System. Chapter 7 - The Pollution Sub-System. Chapter 8 - Energy Resources (Essential reading for chapter 1).
3. Meadows, D. *et al.* (1972). *The Limits to Growth.* London, Earth Island Ltd.
Chapter III - Growth in the World System. IV - Technology and the Limits to Growth.
4. Mesarovic, M. and Pestel, E. (1975). *Mankind at the Turning Point.* London, Hutchinson
A non-technical account of a more recent model, again with references to the technical literature. The whole book is quite readable, but students should find chapters 1, 2, 3, 5, 6, 7 and 9 particularly useful.
5. Roberts, P. (1975). 'The World Can Yet be Saved'. *New Scientist*, 23rd January, pp. 200–201
A very brief account of some of the criticisms which have been made of *Limits of Growth*, and work on rival models.
6. Science Policy Research Unit, Sussex University (1975). *The Art of Anticipation.* Robertson

A very readable collection of articles on the difficulties of coming to grips with the future.

Points for discussion or essays

BASED ON ESSENTIAL READING ONLY

(All of these topics can be dealt with using the essential readings only. If, however, it is wished to supplement the essential readings, relevant material from the list of additional reading is given in brackets after each suggestion.)

What are the difficulties involved in the attainment and the maintenance of an equilibrium state? (4)

All projections of exponential growth eventually lead to absurdity. For instance, there was a time when canal building was growing exponentially, and if people had projected this into the future for ten or twenty years, they would have found that the whole country had been shovelled away to make canals. Why, then, should we take the projections of exponential growth in *Limits to Growth* seriously?

'We do not accept that pollution will necessarily set a limit to economic growth' (*4th Royal Commission Report on Environmental Pollution*, London, HMSO, 1974, p. 4). Discuss. (3)

Why is a regional model of the world preferable to one which cannot deal with regions? (4, 5)

Discuss the sensitivity of a model to assumptions, with special attention to the model used in *Limits to Growth*. Why is sensitivity such an important feature of a model?

Construct a series of feedback loops for public and private transport, university student numbers, the number of strikes, etc.

BASED ON ESSENTIAL AND ADDITIONAL READING

(These topics can only be dealt with using the additional readings as well as the essential ones. The numbers in brackets refer to items on the additional reading list.)

Discuss the role of technological innovation in nullifying the conclusions of *Limits to Growth*. (1, 2, 5)

'The greatest dis-service done to the West by the Arabs was in their not charging *enough* for their oil'. Discuss. (4)

Why is it in the interests of the developed world to help the underdeveloped regions? (4)

Chapter Five
The Technological Fix

Introduction

Can the kind of technology which we have today solve the problems which it has so largely brought about, the problems of resource depletion, pollution and population? This is the question to which this chapter is devoted. Those who think that technology can solve its own problems are said to believe in a 'technological fix'. The debate between this group and its opponents is raging, and looks likely to continue for a long time. In any debate the first party states its case, which is criticized by the second party, and the first party then tries to show that these criticisms are mistaken, and so on. We have tried to capture this to-and-fro of argument by means of a dialogue between FIX, who believes that technology can solve all the problems it has produced, and ANTI-FIX, who denies this.

For convenience the whole debate has been broken into three parts, dealing with resources, pollution and population, although the limitations of this neat division will soon be apparent.

We have not attempted a definitive and complete description of the debate, but give only a sample of the arguments most often met. As the debate continues new points which we have not considered will be raised and what seemed to be major points will fade in importance. This does not, of course, destroy the significance of the debate, for, if truth emerges at all, it emerges only as the result of careful and protracted debate. Discovering the truth is never easy.

Resources

FIX   There are three ways in which technology can continue to provide us with increasing amounts of raw materials; (1) by finding ways of exploiting low grade ores and discovering new deposits; (2) by enabling common materials to be substituted for scarce ones; and (3) by finding ways to conserve our natural resources.
1. As technology advances it will provide us with the means of exploiting lower and lower grades of ore. It will also enable us to gather resources from hitherto inaccessible parts of the globe, such as the deep ocean floors, the Arctic and Antarctic, and deep regions of the crust. Better prospecting techniques can also be expected to add to the reserves of all important resources.

The most pressing of the limits to growth in resource usage are not geological: Mother Nature has put on and in the planet ample for perhaps tens of thousands of years . . . What limits there may be come from man's economic and technological ability to exploit these resources. (W. Page in *Thinking About the Future*, p. 37).

Aluminum provides a striking illustration of how the technology of mining and metallurgy has for practical purposes increased the supply of the metal. Aluminum was first used on a large scale only in the early years of this century. To begin with, manufacture was impeded by the need for ore, called bauxite, which was chemically pure and, in particular, free from silica and iron. Over the years, techniques have been developed for purifying aluminum even in the presence of iron and silica, with the result that it is now possible to extract aluminum from ores that would have been quite useless in the 1930s. As long ago as the early 1960s, the monumental study by Landsberg, Fischman and Fisher, *Resources in America's Future*, estimated that proven world reserves of aluminum ore had doubled from 1600 million tons to 3600 million tons between 1950 and 1958, and that the chemical techniques available at the end of the 1950s made a further 5000 million tons of aluminum ore accessible to the metallurgists. With the development of extraction plants capable of producing large quantities of aluminum metal at great speed, price has become much less dependent than it used to be on the quality of the ore. And now it is likely that the costs of extracting aluminum from ores of all kinds will be reduced by the development of a direct extraction process which avoids one of the expensive intermediate steps in the process. This is why it is no surprise that the price of aluminum metal has fallen gradually for the best part of two decades. Given inflation, this is tantamount to a substantial reduction of real cost, and there is no sign that this trend will be halted. (J. Maddox, *The Doomsday Syndrome*, p. 106).

Reading
Cole H. *et al. Thinking About the Future*, pp. 36—42
Maddox, J. *The Doomsday Syndrome*, pp. 104—107
2. Technology will always enable cheap, common materials to be substituted for expensive, rare ones. An example of this is substitution of aluminum for copper in the electrical industry.

The idea that some materials play such an important part in modern life that civilization would collapse without them is by all criteria an illusion. The most common short list includes

50

naturally occurring substances as different as helium, copper and chromium. In reality, however, all these substances are but means to specific ends. Chromium is an element necessary for making stainless steel, but who would pretend that stainless steel is the only way of manufacturing such things as tableware or vats for the chemical industry? The past few years have shown vividly enough that other materials, synthetic chemicals, for example, can do the same jobs, possibly at greater cost and with less convenience. What this implies is that the objectives of modern industry can usually be attained in several ways by the use of alternative materials. Just as the nuclear-power industry will have to fall back on thorium as a fuel if it ever runs short of uranium, so manufacturers of concrete constructions will be forced to use other metals than steel as reinforcing bars if iron-ore supplies should run out. (J. Maddox, *The Doomsday Syndrome*, p. 108).

Reading:
Maddox, J. *The Doomsday Syndrome*, pp. 107–110
3. Technology will enable much of our processed raw materials to be recycled. For example, the steel industry already uses a great deal of scrap, but it cannot use tin cans because the lining of tin must first be removed and this is too expensive. If the tins were coated with a suitable resin, instead of tin, they could be recycled. These resins already exist; it is merely a question of organizing our resources properly.

ANTI-FIX   Your arguments ignore the problem of energy. All of these remedies to the problem of resources fall down because of energy considerations. Taking them in turn:
1. The processing of low grade ore requires far more energy than the processing of rich ore. New methods for exploiting hitherto untouched regions of the earth will also require large amounts of energy. For example, much more energy will be needed to extract metal ores from deep within the earth's crust than is used in traditional mining.
2. It seems to be the case that when one material is used as a substitute for another, the substitute consumes far more energy in its manufacture than the original. The energy needed for the production of natural fibres, such as cotton and wool, comes from the sun; either directly or through food eaten by the animal producing the fibre. Energy for the production of synthetic fibres, however, must be supplied from burning oil, gas or coal. Production of nylon, for instance, involves a series of chemical reactions which require temperatures between 95–375°C, involving considerable fuel consumption.

3. Recycling energy involves a breach of the fundamental laws of thermodynamics, and so is impossible. Nevertheless energy, often in large quantities, is needed for the collection of waste and its treatment to produce re-usable materials. One way of dealing with scrap cars, for instance, is the removal of plastic trimmings, tyres, seats etc. to leave a hulk which is then smashed to pieces. Ferrous metals are removed by a magnet, and non-ferrous metals are sorted manually. The smashing machine requires 20kw hours of energy per car. In another process the hulk is heated to progressively higher temperatures, the metals melting in order of their melting points and being collected separately. The energy consumed here is obviously quite large.

There are two consequences of the above points:

1. There are not likely to be enough energy reserves to provide industry with the materials it needs.
2. Even if there were sufficient reserves of energy in the world, they would soon be consumed at such a rate as to create serious heat pollution.

Readings:

Chapman, P. (1973). 'No Overdrafts in Energy Economics'. *New Scientist*, 17th May

Commoner, B. *The Closing Circle*, pp. 158–61 and 172–3

Diamant, R. *The Prevention of Pollution*, pp. 66–7

FIX   We'll take up the question of heat pollution in the next section. Let us concentrate on resources for the moment. You forget that technology can provide all the energy we shall need to expand our consumption of natural resources. Who, just a hundred years ago, could have foreseen the coming of oil as an important fuel, or the development of nuclear power? And do not forget the possibility of exploiting non-exhaustable energy sources, such as sunlight, wind and wave power.

> With present techniques, the equivalent of 10 000 tons of coal can be won from each ton of uranium; in the 1980s, the conversion rate will be something more like 10 000 000 tons of coal from each ton of uranium. Moreover, nuclear reactors will be able to use materials other than uranium, thorium perhaps. The development of nuclear energy in the past 20 years has increased ten fold the amount of energy that could economically be extracted from the earth's crust. The prospect . . . of a crippling scarcity of energy has been exorcised by a single technological development. (J. Maddox, *The Doomsday Syndrome*, p. 100).

> If only a few percent of the land area of the US could be used to absorb solar radiation effectively (at, say, a little better than 10% efficiency), we would meet most of our energy needs

in the year 2000. (C. Starr, 1971) 'Energy and Power',
Scientific American, September).

Reading:
Hunt, S. *Fission, Fusion and the Energy Crisis,* Chapters 7 and 8
Hill, P. and Vievoye, R. *Energy in Crisis,* Chapter 9
ANTI-FIX   This brings us back to problems about the environment.
Many who look to technology to supply the vast quantities of energy
we will require in the future base their faith on nuclear power.
Nuclear reactors may be able to provide this energy, but their wastes
must be stored under controlled conditions for something like
250 000 years (and some say much longer − 100 million years). This
is an impossible burden to pass on to future generations.
Reading:
Sixth Report of the Royal Commission on Environmental Pollution
FIX   But then technology will find a way of dealing with these
wastes. Since we seem to have got onto environmental issues, perhaps
we should talk about them in a general way.

Pollution

FIX   Technology can provide the solution for all pollution problems. In a review of modern anti-pollution techniques, Diamant
states that:

> . . . our technology, which causes many of our pollution
> problems, is equally well able to solve them; techniques already
> exist for reducing pollution, from virtually every source, to
> negligible proportions. These techniques are not in widespread
> use because, in most countries, there is no compulsion to use
> them . . . . It is the author's belief that within a few years the
> governments of most countries will pass very stringent laws
> regarding the state of the environment. (*The Prevention of
> Pollution,* pp. 1–3)

As industry grows overall pollution can only be kept low if the
pollution per unit of production is reduced at the same rate as output increases. This is, however, quite possible. As industry produces
more and more wealth, it can afford to invest in ever improving anti-
pollution devices. Anyway, removing some kinds of pollution can be
directly profitable.

> What the public must come to accept . . . is a modest increase
> in the price to be paid for goods and services to cover the
> costs of avoiding pollution. For example . . . installation of

sulfur dioxide scrubbers in the chimneys of power stations and factories will certainly add a little to the price of electricity and the goods manufactured. The *pace of rationalization and technological progress in industry is such that the additional cost could soon be offset by increased efficiency.* But in many fields of environmental improvement, including prevention of air pollution, reduction of water-borne diseases, and incineration rather than dumping of solid refuse, there could be direct cash benefits to the community. (R. Diamant, *The Prevention of Pollution*, pp. 2–3)

Reading:
Diamant, R. *The Prevention of Pollution*, Chapter 1 and pp. 211–244
Marstrand, P. and Sinclair, T. 'The Pollution Sub-System', Chapter 7
    Thinking About the Future, edited by H. Cole *et al.*
ANTI-FIX   Technology, by itself, cannot produce a clean environment, for a fundamental change in our whole economic system is needed first. In a capitalist economy each producer tries to make as much profit as he can, but spending money on anti-pollution devices brings him no return. If it is a choice between spending money here, and buying new machinery, the producer will always buy new machinery, because he can make profit from what it can produce.

> Industrial concerns exist not to serve people but to make profits. As this entails that the greatest return should be expected for the minimum investment, the attitude towards pollution control is that it is money spent without return. (*Industry Week*, 1969. 5th December, p. 27).

It is no good one country passing anti-pollution laws to make its industrialists conform to public wishes because, more often than not, the industrialist is competing with foreign firms. If he has to spend money controlling pollution whilst his competitors do not, his product will be uneconomic and non-competitive. As H. Doan, the President of the Dow Chemical Co. of the USA has stated:

> Industry already lives in one world. We compete globally. The United States and all its problems will not do well unless industry is competitive. As a nation, we are not free to assign costs where we will. We are somewhat captive of economic practice in other parts of the world. Our society already assesses more costs to industry in the form of taxes than any other country by a wide margin . . . It is only our enormous productivity that keeps us still competitive. To say this another way, if all countries put the burden of pollution costs on their industry, we could handle these costs too. If they don't — and

they don't now and aren't likely to in the future . . . then we can't either.

Nor can we hope for international agreement on pollution legislation. Some country is almost always certain to have a vested interest in allowing its industry to be polluting (e.g. when it has industries which have heavily invested in now outdated plants which can only be competitive by producing pollution).
Reading:
Commoner, B. *The Closing Circle*, Chapter 11, pp. 250–292
Rothman, H. *Murderous Providence*, pp. 298–308
Mishan, F. *The Cost of Economic Growth*
FIX   Despite all these difficulties pollution controls *have been* introduced, nowhere more so than in the USA, the bastion of free enterprise. For example, in California very strict laws on air pollution succeeded, over a period of 8 years, in reducing particulate emissions from oil refineries from 12 tonnes per 100 000 tonnes refinery capacity, to almost nil, and reduced sulfur dioxide and hydrocarbon emission by three-quarters and a half respectively.
Reading:
Diamant R. *The Prevention of Pollution*, Chapter 2
Rothman, H. *Murderous Providence*, Chapter 19
Fourth Report of the Royal Commission on Environmental Pollution, Chapter 3, pp. 58–66
Control of Pollution Act, 1974
ANTI-FIX   Leaving these political questions, there are three kinds of pollution which technology cannot deal with: 1. unexpected pollutants; 2. long-lived pollutants; and 3. waste heat.
1. It may be possible for technology to deal with known and recognized pollutants, but it is possible for chemicals thought to be harmless, or thought to exist in only harmless quantities, to do great, and possibly irreversible, damage to the ecosphere. For instance, it now appears that the halocarbon gases which are used in aerosol cans may have damaged the upper atmosphere by lowering its ozone concentration. Ozone is important because it filters out harmful ultraviolet radiation from the sun's light. It is likely that combinations of food additives and pollutants, relatively harmless by themselves, can be harmful in combination. An experimental search for such harmful combinations is almost impossible. Also concentration of these substances now thought harmless may in future be bound to be damaging. These considerations may be relevant to the high incidence of so-called diseases of civilization.
Reading:
'Aerosol Sprays and the Ozone Shield', *New Scientist* (1974), 5th December, pp. 717–720

2. There is no technological solution to the problem of very long-term pollutants. Chief amongst these is the waste from nuclear power stations. Here, energy is derived from the fission of uranium 235 or plutonium 239 atoms. After some time the fuel in such a reactor contains so much useless products of this fission that it must be removed from the reactor. The waste products are separated and the remaining fuel reformed and returned to the reactor. Many of the waste products are, however, highly radio-active, some having half-lives of several thousand years. It may be that these long-lived wastes must be stored for thousands of years before their radioactivity has died away to safe levels.

Reading:
Rothman, H. *Murderous Providence*, pp. 211–217 and 232–233
Sixth Report of the Royal Commission on Environmental Pollution

3. Technology can give us no way of dealing with waste heat. The quantity of heat produced by industry will eventually be so large that it will interfere with the delicate balance of the earth's climate. Any large scale change in climate is very likely to be harmful to animal and plant life, agriculture and directly to man. If energy consumption grows at something like its present rate for the next 75 years, it will be about 60 times its present level. It has been calculated that this will lead to an overall temperature increase of 0.3 °C. This may seem small enough, but we know very little about the delicate balance of the earth's climate, and such an increase may tip this balance in an irreversible way.

Reading:
Rothman, H. *Murderous Providence*, pp. 204–5

FIX   All I can say about your three kinds of intractable pollution problem is that 1. we must carefully screen all chemicals that are likely to find their way into the environment; 2. we will find ways of disposing of radioactive wastes; and 3. there is no problem of waste heat. There is no real problem of heat pollution, since the heat generated by man's activities is only a tiny fraction of that supplied by the sun. In the UK, one of the most densely industrialized countries in the world, heat energy produced by man accounts for only about 0.75% of the total solar energy received by the land and air over the country.

> Taking the large tracts of sea and unpopulated land into account, it seems clear that it will be a very long time before direct thermal pollution of the environment reaches the point at which it would have a detectable effect on world climate. (*First Report of the Royal Commission on Environmental Pollution*, p. 41)

Population

FIX   Technology will provide us with socially acceptable contraceptives which will reduce the birth rate in underdeveloped countries.
For instance, Weinberg says of the interuterine device or coil (IUD):

> Probably the most important new Technological Fix is the
> intrauterine device for birth control. Before the IUD was
> invented, birth control demanded very strong motivation of
> countless individuals. Even with the pill, the individual's moti-
> vation had to be sustained day in and day out; should it flag
> even temporarily, the strong motivation of the previous month
> might go for naught. But the IUD, being a one-shot method,
> greatly reduces the individual motivation required to induce a
> social change. To be sure, the mother must be sufficiently
> motivated to accept the IUD in the first place, but, as experi-
> ence in India already seems to show, it is much easier to
> persuade the Indian mother to accept the IUD once than it is
> to persuade her to take a pill every day. The IUD does not
> completely replace social engineering by technology: indeed, in
> some Spanish American cultures where the husband's manliness
> is measured by the number of children he has, the IUD attacks
> only part of the problem. Yet in many other situations, as in
> India, the IUD so reduces the social component of the problem
> as to make an impossibly difficult social problem much less
> hopeless. (In *Man Made Futures*, p. 284).

Reading:
Ehrlich, P. and Ehrlich, A. *Population, Resources, Environment,*
    pp. 236–57
Myrdal, G. *The Challenge of World Poverty,* Chapter 5
ANTI-FIX   Birth control facilities are not enough for they merely
enable a woman to have as many children as she and her husband
wish. Attention must be paid first to the social, economic, cultural
and religious factors which determine family size in underdeveloped
countries. The magnitude of the problem can be seen from the table
in *Population, Resources, Environment,* p. 239.
FIX   Yes, people must be given an incentive for smaller families,
but technology can give them just this. As technology increases the
wealth of people living in underdeveloped countries, the populations
of these countries will undergo the demographic transition to a low
birth rate and low death rate, just as European countries did in the
past. This is because, as wealth increases, children become more and
more of an economic burden on their parents. This is a common
argument of the governments of underdeveloped countries — that

their country's population problems are not to be solved by birth control programs, but by greater affluence. A Committee for Economic Development report on the population of Latin America stated, for instance:

> Population is growing faster in Latin America than anywhere else in the world. Naturally, this slows the increase of *per capita* gross national product. Yet this fact should not be considered decisive. Much less can it be used to propose birth control, or, more euphemistically, family planning, as a solution . . . Latin American experience demonstrates that this is not the main factor . . . the solution is not birth control but increased food production and economic development, which brings about higher productivity and therefore a higher standard of living.

Reading:
Commoner, B. *The Closing Circle*, pp. 232–249
Maddox, J. *The Doomsday Syndrome*, pp. 48–64
Cassen, R. 'Economic Demographic Interrelationships.' In *Population and its Problems*, ed. by H. Parry.

ANTI-FIX   Technology offers no solution to the population problem, since growing population effectively prevents the accumulation of wealth needed to fund new industries and services. Thus the poor countries' growing populations prevent technology from generating wealth for them. *Before* this can happen, birth rates must be lowered. Thus a report from the Committee for Economic Development stated that:

> The experience of the past decade offers convincing evidence that if low income countries are to develop rapidly they must avoid or extricate themselves from the 'population trap', by which we mean rates of increase of population growth so large that they approach the feasible rates of increase in economic output, thereby preventing significant growth in *per capita* output . . . To meet the population problem effectively, programs of family planning must play a part.

Reading:
Donaldson, P. *Worlds Apart*
Ehrlich, P. and Ehrlich, A. *Population, Resources, Environment,* Chapter 10

FIX   Fortunately, figures do not bear you out. Standards of living in nearly all developing countries are increasing, and the birth rate in many of them shows a clear downward trend. It looks, therefore, as though rising living standards are reducing family size.

58

Reading:
UN Demographic Yearbooks
UN Statistical Yearbooks
ANTI-FIX   But you are forgetting the problem of resources. There are simply not enough natural resources in the world for the standard of living of the underdeveloped countries to be raised to a level sufficient for the demographic transition to occur. Even if this were possible, the global pollution produced would be too great, and would interfere irreversibly with some part of the ecosystem on which mankind depends for its very existence.

There are many reasons why most UDCs cannot (and should not) be industrialized along DC lines. The most impressive constraints are probably the environmental ones, especially those associated with pollution, and thermal limits. As one biologist put it, 'Just think of what would happen to the atmosphere if 700 million Chinese started driving big automobiles!' But even below these limits it seems highly unlikely that the problems posed by the depletion of non-renewable resources would permit more than a very limited industrial development of most UDCs, unless, of course, there were some sort of massive de-industrialization of most DCs. (P. and A. Ehrlich, *Population, Resources, Environment,* p. 300).

Reading:
Meadows, D. *et al. Limits to Growth*
This is especially true of energy. Technology may provide us with high-yielding varieties of crops and the like, but such improvements in food production are heavily dependent on energy. There simply will not be enough energy to produce all the food the world is going to need.

Table 6   Average energy inputs in corn production in USA (kcal x 10^3 per acre)

Input	1945	1950	1954	1959	1964	1970
Machinery	180	250	300	350	420	420
Irrigation	19	23	27	31	34	34
Drying	10	30	60	100	120	120
Electricity	32	54	100	140	203	310
Transport	20	30	45	60	70	70
Yield (bushel per acre)	34	38	41	54	68	81

(D. Pimental *et al.,* 1973. 'Food Production and the Energy Crisis', *Science,* **182,** pp. 443—448. Copyright 1973 by the American Association for the Advancement of Science)

FIX   Technological development of new plant varieties may eliminate the need for large quantities of fertilizer. Borlaug, for example,

59

envisages the production of cereal varieties with nitrogen-fixing nodules attached to their roots, thus obviating the need for at least nitrogenous fertilizers. Technology can also provide new forms of energy at low cost.

Reading:

Borlaug, N. (1971). 'The Green Revolution'. *Bulletin of the Atomic Scientists*, pp. 6–9 and 42–49.

The arguments must remain inconclusive and the debate could be extended almost indefinitely. Which side is right is not an easy judgment to make, but surely without ANTI-FIX, FIX would be less likely to succeed in controlling the ill-effects of technology; indeed, he might not even try.

Points for discussion or essays

It is suggested that students be given some part of the dialogue to investigate in depth, using the readings mentioned. These often duplicate reading for earlier chapters, though this should be an advantage, reinforcing the student's understanding of the issues.

Chapter Six
Appropriate Technology

Intermediate technology and development

All too often when we think of technology, we think only of
western, large scale, centralized, capital and energy intensive technology. It is only possible for such a technology to exist in a society
where a whole host of special conditions are satisfied. For example,
people must be prepared to sell their labor for money; workers must
regulate their activities closely by the clock; at least some people must
be educated, some of them to very high standards; there must exist
towns and large cities to provide the workers needed in centralized
factories; these must be fed by intensive farming in the rural areas;
and good communications must exist between town and country so
that food can be transported easily. Road and rail links are essential,
because many products will need to be processed in several factories
before they are finished; there must be markets for the goods produced, and people trained to seek out and exploit new markets for
their products. Since the educational system and the roads and railways generally need support from public funds, there must also exist
an efficient system of tax gathering and disbursement, and so on and
so on. Whilst the kind of technology we find in developed countries
may be appropriate to these countries, because all these conditions are
met, it will not necessarily be appropriate to other, less developed
countries where many of these requirements may be missing. Possibly
quite *different types* of technology will be appropriate to the less
developed countries.

Indeed it is often argued that western technology is inappropriate
to underdeveloped countries and that western aid should not concentrate on helping underdeveloped countries to acquire the kind of
technology developed countries rely on. The following reasons are
used to support this claim.

1. Western technology is capital intensive. That is, it uses lots of
   expensive machinery and little labor. It therefore can do very
   little to reduce unemployment, which we have seen to be a very
   serious problem in many underdeveloped countries.
2. Large-scale industrial units need to be located in or near large
   towns or cities to draw their labor, and so can make little or no
   contribution to the major problem of rural underemployment.
3. Western technology depends on a supply of highly skilled labor
   of all kinds, from skilled manual workers to managers. These
   cannot be provided by most underdeveloped countries. For this
   reason imported plant is either run extremely inefficiently, because

of lack of skilled manpower, or else its running depends upon a team of foreign experts.

4. Western technology is extremely expensive and its import by an underdeveloped country means a significant drain on its foreign reserves.

5. The importing of western methods of production produces a great divide between rich, well paid, (and often unionized) city workers, and the poor farmers in the rural areas.

6. The products of the imported, western-style technology are often only saleable abroad. If they are saleable in the home market, the effect is merely to make unemployed those workers producing the same items by traditional methods. Western technology can, therefore, lead to a net *loss* of jobs in an underdeveloped country. If this is avoided by exporting the products, the benefits do not go directly to the local community, but to private owners or the state. The products must also compete with similar ones produced in developed countries.

For these reasons, Schumacher has suggested that a far more appropriate kind of technology for underdeveloped countries is what he calls 'intermediate' technology. Intermediate technology is defined in terms of cost of equipment per worker. Calling the indigenous, inadequate technology a '£1' technology, and that of the developed countries a '£1000' technology, intermediate technology is called a '£100' technology. In other words, the cost per workplace for intermediate technology lies between the cost per workplace for the indigenous technology, and that for western technology. As an example we might consider ploughing. The indigenous technology may accomplish this using primitive hand tools, whilst western technology uses sophisticated tractors. Intermediate technology, on the other hand, might provide efficient animal-drawn tools, or, at greater cost, a plough drawn by a fixed winch, operated by a simple internal combustion engine. In the generation of power, indigenous technology may use little more than animal effort, whilst western technology makes use of enormous power stations. Intermediate technology would provide small generating units using whatever energy sources were available locally, peat, coal or water, for instance (see Sigurdson, 1973).

Schumacher claims that intermediate technology is appropriate for underdeveloped countries for the following reasons.

1. For the same cost, intermediate technology provides far more jobs than does western technology, although it is less productive. It is right, in these countries, to sacrifice output for jobs, as the problems of unemployment are so serious.

2. It does not need to be situated in towns and so can help stem the flood of people leaving the countryside for the towns.

3. The principles exploited by intermediate technology are simple

and so it can be understood by most people who use it. It does not need foreign experts.

4. Intermediate technology can be used to produce goods for the home market without displacing traditional workers, since they can afford to buy the equipment needed (perhaps with the aid of government loans). More money is paid in wages for workers in intermediate technology than in western technology, and this money goes straight into the local community where it can circulate to everybody's benefit.

Not every task, however, may be suitable for intermediate technology. For things such as steel and chemical manufacture, and land reclamation, imported technologies may be most appropriate, whilst the tractor is essential for some agricultural tasks in certain areas. Intermediate technology does not necessarily attempt to displace western technology. Instead the two can be seen as partners; as two different technologies appropriate to two quite different social and economic situations. Moreover intermediate technology may be dependent upon western technology for some of its materials (e.g. iron and steel, aluminum, petroleum, chemicals etc.). We must also note that the distinction between the two kinds of technology is not an absolute one, for they shade into one another. In one country the kind of technology that is appropriate may be a '£100' technology, against the '£1000' technology of the developed countries, whilst in another a '£200' or '£400' technology may be the most appropriate. It is arbitrary, of course, whether we call such a '£400' technology a primitive western style one, or a sophisticated variety of intermediate technology.

Appropriate technology for developed countries

We have seen that intermediate technology has been advocated for developing countries. It is thought that their particular circumstances of shortage of capital, shortage of foreign currency and availability of labor, make intermediate technology eminently suitable for them. It may be argued, however, that the principles underlying the ideas for intermediate technology are equally appropriate for modifications to western technology.

If we wish to escape the many problems brought about by modern technological developments, we must re-think some of the criteria implicit in the choice of our technologies. Such new criteria for western technology have been proposed by several authors. Braun has suggested three main new criteria for design: efficient use of materials in production; efficient use of products; easy recirculation of materials. Goods must be made from the minimum of natural resources, especially scarce ones. The production of waste, especially harmful waste, must be kept to a minimum and all waste must be efficiently disposed of. Efficient disposal will reduce pollution and increase recirculation of useful materials. Goods must be designed so as to last as long as possible and so that their materials content can be easily recirculated when their useful life comes to an end. Energy must be used as sparingly as possible.

It has been shown by the authors of *Limits to Growth* (chapter 4) that similar criteria can have a stabilizing effect on the world economic systems as modelled by them. They stress, however, that the stabilization of population is a pre-condition of the success of any technological and agricultural changes.

Any change in technology involves change in society. Many of these changes are often unforeseen, and it has been advocated by many authors that more attention should be paid to the wider social implications of any technology before it is adopted. Any attempt to do this has become known as Technology Assessment. This has many definitions, of which we shall quote but one, used in the Congressional Research Service of the American Library of Congress:

> Technology assessment is the process of taking a purposeful look at the consequences of technological change. It includes the primary cost/benefit balance of short-term localized market place economics, but particularly goes beyond these to identify affected parties and unanticipated impacts in as broad and long range fashion as is possible. It is neutral and objective, seeking to enrich the information for management decisions. Both 'good' and 'bad' side effects are investigated since a missed opportunity for benefit may be detrimental to society just as is an unexpected hazard.

The details of the many techniques used for technology assessment are beyond the scope of this book. It is significant, however, that much thought is now being given to modifications of western technologies which would enable advanced technological societies to survive and improve, despite the hazards reviewed.

> During this century technology has become the dominant force in the shaping of societies. But how much do we know about its capabilities, its long-term effects and the methods we can use to control and direct it?
>
> Some form of technology assessment has always existed. Firms have always undertaken investigations to find out whether their products will sell. This activity developed into technological forecasting and market research. Equally, the government has always regulated the side effects of technology by legislation

on pollution, safety and usage. In recent years it has influenced technological development increasingly by subsidies from public funds for research and development. We have now reached a stage when practically all major technological innovation depends upon government funding.

Yet despite all this, technology has persisted with the nasty habit of turning up unforeseen and unpleasant side effects, has perpetually failed to answer some of the more urgent problems of the day and has continually ignored long term processes.

We apply no end of double standards. On the one hand we hail a major investment in the car industry as a breakthrough towards the millenium, on the other hand we acknowledge that a tolerable urban environment is incompatible with the un-restricted use of the motor car and that the world reserves of natural fuels are running out rapidly.

Technology Assessment cannot avoid all these pitfalls, but it can help by clarifying and foreseeing some of them. Technology Assessment cannot replace the political processes of reaching decisions on social and economic problems. It can, however, provide insight into some or all of the following questions:

1. What are the likely total effects of the introduction of a given technology? By total effects we mean the effects on natural resources, on pollution, on transport, on social customs and habits, on work satisfaction, on the visual and audible environment, on leisure. This kind of study can be undertaken on the grand scale for, say, the channel tunnel or the fast breeder reactor. It can also be undertaken on a much smaller scale for, say, double glazing in houses or solid state electronics in telephone exchanges.
2. What are the technologies that need to be developed to achieve identified social objectives, such as the long term supply of energy and raw materials, the alleviation of congestion, the provision of housing, and of a clean and healthy environment?

To achieve an effective policy for technology, it is necessary to understand how decisions about technology are made both in private enterprise and in the public sector. The control of technology involves management of R & D, public investment, legislation, committees and ministries, funding mechanisms, public enquiries and pressure groups.

The main differences between the newly emerging discipline of Technology Assessment and its predecessors are the breadth of context in which technology is considered and the time scale on which it is viewed.

The direct consequence of these differences, especially the former, is the necessity to form interdisciplinary teams of varying composition for each technology assessment or technology policy problem. It is impossible for any one person to have the breadth of knowledge and the breadth of approach required to provide answers of any profundity to the problems raised. It will take, (to mention but a few) lawyers and engineers, technologists and economists, planners and sociologists, chemists and psychologists, systems analysts and physicists, operational researchers and political scientists, to be involved in varying degrees. (E. Braun 'Does Technology Mean Progress', *Aston Observer*).

Technology Assessment is not the cure for all ills, but it may help decision makers to make sensible technological choices and thus avoid the doom so often forecast.

In the view of many thinkers on contemporary problems, modifications suggested by proper assessment of technology and the use of new criteria such as set out above, should sufficiently change attitudes and patterns of consumption and pollution to make the survival of advanced societies perfectly feasible. There are those, however, who argue that resource depletion, pollution and over-population, cannot be solved within existing economic, social and political frameworks. Their answer to these problems involves radical changes in all aspects of contemporary western life, and a return to an existence less dependent upon sophisticated technology and more in harmony with nature. For them, man should not try to dominate nature using western technology, but should cooperate with it, using small scale, less disruptive, intermediate technology. Another advantage of a wholesale change to intermediate technology, according to this group, is that society can be 'decentralized'. The large-scale production of western technology calls for large urban communities to provide its labor force, and can only function in a society where economic and political control is concentrated in the hands of a government whose power extends over millions of people. Intermediate technology, on the other hand, can operate properly only in small communities which are more or less self-sufficient, and so able to be more or less self-governing. Cities should not exist because they need large-scale sewerage systems, transport networks, water and fuel services etc., which cannot be provided by the tools of intermediate technology and their elimination is seen as a great benefit. Living in modern cities, it is argued, leads to social disruption, whose symptoms we can see in climbing rates for crime, suicide, mental illness, alcoholism and other social diseases.

One exponent of this view has painted the following picture of a society which has freed itself from the tyranny of western technology, and depends only upon intermediate technology:

A countryside dotted with windmills and solar houses, studded
with intensively but organically-worked plots of lands; food
production systems dependent on the integration of many
different species, with timber, fish, animals and plants playing
mutually dependent roles; with wilderness areas plentifully
available . . . ; a life-style for men and women which involved
hard physical work but not over-excessively long hours or in a
tediously repetitive way; . . . a political system so decentralized
and small that individuals — all individuals — could play more
than a formal, once-every five years role. (R. Clarke, 1973.
'Technology for an Alternative Society'. *New Scientist*, January
11th.)

A study entitled *Blueprint for Survival* suggests a plan for bringing
about the transformation of western society to an intermediate technological society.

Reading

ESSENTIAL

Clarke, R. (1973). 'The Pressing Need for Alternative Technology'.
  Impact of Science on Society, XXIII, No. 4, Oct—Dec. pp.
  257—271, reprinted in *Man Made Futures*, edited by N. Cross, D.
  Elliott and R. Roy. pp. 31—38 and 333—339. London, Hutchinson
  (1974)
  Argues that the only solution to the problems of resource
  depletion, pollution and alienation is the return to a more primitive kind of society which employs intermediate or alternative
  technology. He gives several examples of how devices of an
  intermediate technology can be used to avoid pollution, waste and
  agricultural decline.
Gibbons, M. (1973). 'Technology Assessment'. *New Scientist*, June
  A brief introduction to the subject for the layman.
Ibezim, M. O. (1974). 'Planning for the Future'. *Appropriate
  Technology*, 1, 1, pp. 18—19
  An excellent short account of intermediate technology and its
  impact on underdeveloped countries, especially African ones.
  There will always be some need for western-style technology,
  however.
Schumacher, E. (1973). *Small is Beautiful*. London, Blond and
  Briggs
  The classical account of the need for intermediate technology in
  underdeveloped countries. The concept 'intermediate technology'

first appears in this work. Essential reading is Part I; Chapter 1,
Part III; Chapters 1, 2 and 4.

ADDITIONAL

1. *A Blueprint for Survival* (1972). London, Penguin (first appeared
   as Vol 2, No. 1, of *The Ecologist*), Chapters 1, 2 and 3.
   An outline of the need for a decentralized system using only
   intermediate technology and proposals for how this kind of
   society can be brought into being.
2. Bhalla, A. and Baron, C. (1974). 'Appropriate Technology,
   Poverty and Unemployment: The ILO Project'. *Appropriate
   Technology I*, 4, pp. 20–22.
   A brief account of the ILO project which aims to provide
   developing countries with technology which is appropriate to them.
3. Braun, E. (1972). 'Safeguarding the Environment'. *Technology and
   Society*, 7, 4, pp. 134–136.
   Using a model relating resources, manufacture, consumption and
   recycling, criteria for conservation of resources are suggested.
4. Charles, K. (1974). 'Intermediate Technology, Can it Work?'
   Appropriate Technology I, 4, pp. 14–15.
   A very brief account of some of the problems facing the introduction of intermediate technology into underdeveloped countries
   and the way in which developed countries can help.
5. Clarke, R. (1973). 'Technology for an Alternative Society'. *New
   Scientist*, 11th January.
   A very brief statement of the problems created by traditional
   technology and how they can only be solved by an 'alternative
   society' based on intermediate technology.
6. Dickson, D. (1974). *Alternative Technology*. London, Fontana
   Chapter 6
   Intermediate technology is not a cure-all for the problems
   produced by traditional technology. It can only be effective
   within a radically different political framework – an alternative
   society.
7. Hetman, F. (1973). *Society and the Assessment of Technology*.
   Paris, OECD
   A detailed account of the purpose, organization and methodology
   used for the assessment of technology.
8. Jackson, S. 'Economically Appropriate Technologies for Developing Countries: A Survey', (available from Overseas Development
   Council, 1717 Massachusetts Avenue, NW, Washington DC 20036,
   USA)
   Examines the relevance of technologies to the economic situations
   of various developing countries. She analyzes arguments for and
   against importing western technologies, and developing intermediate ones. An annotated bibliography is also included.

9. Jéquier, M. (1976). *Appropriate Technology*. Paris, OECD
   An up-to-date account of problems and possibilities together with descriptions of several technological projects.
10. Marsden, K. (1970). 'Progressive Technologies for Developing Countries'. *International Labor Review*, **101**, pp. 475–502.
    An excellent article on the need for appropriate technology in underdeveloped countries — with many case-studies on the failures of imported western technology. Criteria for judging the appropriateness of a technological innovation are discussed.
11. Schumacher, E. (1973). *Small is Beautiful*. London, Blond & Briggs.
    A development of the ideas contained in the Chapters mentioned in the list of essential reading. Part I, Chapters 3 and 4 — an attack on standard economics which regards items such as fresh air and clean water as free, and attaches no cost to pollution. It needs to be replaced by what Schumacher calls a 'Buddhist' economics which will consider such factors. Part II, Chapters 2, 3 and 4 — a discussion of resources, both industrial and agricultural, and our profligate use of them.
12. Sigurdson, J. (1973). 'The Suitability of Technology in Contemporary China'. *Impact of Science on Society*, XXIII, 4, Oct–Dec. pp. 341–352
    An interesting account of the kind of small scale technology being developed in China.
13. Williams, R. (1971). *Politics and Technology*. London, Macmillan
    A brief survey of the many problems posed to politics by technological possibilities.
14. The journal *Appropriate Technology* can be consulted for examples of intermediate technology.

Points for discussion or essays

BASED ON ESSENTIAL READING ONLY

(All of these topics can be dealt with using the essential readings only. If, however, it is wished to supplement the essential reading, relevant material from the list of additional reading is given in brackets after each suggestion.)

Is intermediate technology appropriate to western society? (1, 5, 6)

Could intermediate technology be substituted for western technology without changes in society so drastic as to be revolutionary? (1, 5, 6)

We have seen that technologies form a spectrum, with western technology at one end, and the technology of primitive tribes at the other. How can we decide the most appropriate technology from this spectrum, in a given situation? (It may be helpful for the teacher to suggest various examples, such as the technology of sewage disposal, or canal digging etc.) (7, 8, 10, 11, 12)

What criticisms have been made against the introduction of intermediate technology into underdeveloped countries? What do you think of these criticisms? (8, 10, 11)

In the kind of society envisaged by the proponents of world-wide intermediate technology, there will be no economic growth. They also claim that, in this society, people will be free of the exploitation which western technology imposes on people. Kenneth Boulding, however, has argued that these two features are inconsistent, and that frictions between rich and poor can only be increased in a society with no economic growth:

> In the progressive state, conflicts can be resolved easily by progress itself. The poor can get richer without the rich getting poorer. In the stationary state, if the poor are to get richer, then the rich must get poorer, and what is even more frightening, if the rich are to get richer, they can only do so by increasing their exploitation of the poor, and since the rich may be the most powerful, they may have strong incentives to do this.

Discuss.
('On Problems of Public Policy'. In *Energy, Economic Growth and the Environment*. Edited by S. Schurr. pp. 149–50). (1, 5, 6)

BASED ON ESSENTIAL AND ADDITIONAL READING

(These topics can only be dealt with using the additional readings as well as the essential ones. The numbers in brackets refer to items on the additional reading list.)

Is the *Blueprint for Survival* a Utopian document, and if it is, what is its value? (1)

What can be learned from cases where western technology has been mis-applied in underdeveloped countries? (8, 10, 11)

Discuss the present Chinese attitude towards technology. Can we learn anything from this? (12)

In the proposed transition from our present society to one wholly based upon intermediate technology, what are we to do with the enormous invested wealth represented by our cities, factories, roads, railways, sewers, etc, etc? (1)

Can Technology Assessment solve the problems created by technology in advanced countries? (7, 13)